Workshop on Novel Computational Approaches to Keyphrase Extraction 2015

Co-located with ACL-IJCNLP 2015

Beijing, China
30 July 2015

ISBN: 978-1-5108-0954-3

Printed from e-media with permission by:

Curran Associates, Inc.
57 Morehouse Lane
Red Hook, NY 12571

Some format issues inherent in the e-media version may also appear in this print version.

Printed by Curran Associates, Inc. (2015)

For permission requests, please contact the Association for Computational Linguistics at the address below.

Association for Computational Linguistics
209 N. Eighth Street
Stroudsburg, Pennsylvania 18360

Phone: 1-570-476-8006
Fax: 1-570-476-0860

acl@aclweb.org

Additional copies of this publication are available from:

Curran Associates, Inc.
57 Morehouse Lane
Red Hook, NY 12571 USA
Phone: 845-758-0400
Fax: 845-758-2634
Email: curran@proceedings.com
Web: www.proceedings.com

ACL-IJCNLP 2015

Proceedings of the ACL 2015 Workshop on Novel Computational Approaches to Keyphrase Extraction

July 30, 2015
Beijing, China

Preface

The ACL 2015 Workshop on Novel Computational Approaches to Keyphrase Extraction was held on July 30, 2015 in Beijing, China as part of the 53rd annual meeting of the ACL and the 7th International Joint Conference on Natural Language Processing.

The workshop's goal was to bring together researchers addressing a wide-range of questions pertaining to the keyphrase extraction task as well as domain-specific applications involving the use of keyphrases.

The workshop program included two invited talks by researchers who are experts in the fields of data mining, information retrieval, and natural language processing: Prof. Min-Yen Kan from National University of Singapore and Dr. Preslav Nakov, senior scientist at Qatar Computing Research Institute.

After a rigorous review process, two long papers and three short papers were selected for inclusion into the workshop proceedings by the Program Committee. We hope that these papers summarize novel findings related to keyphrase extraction and invoke further research interest on this exciting topic.

We thank the authors, invited speakers, program committee members, and participants for sharing their research ideas and valuable time to be part of ACL Keyphrase!

–Organizers: Sujatha Das Gollapalli, Cornelia Caragea, Xiaoli Li, C. Lee Giles

Organizers:

Sujatha Das Gollapalli, Institute for Infocomm Research, A*STAR, Singapore
Cornelia Caragea, University of North Texas, USA
Xiaoli Li, Institute for Infocomm Research, A*STAR, Singapore
C. Lee Giles, The Pennsylvania State University, USA

Program Committee:

Marina Danilevsky, IBM Almaden Research Center
Fei Liu, Carnegie Mellon University
Doina Caragea, Kansas State University
Rada Mihalcea, University of Michigan
Shibamouli Lahiri, University of Michigan
Saurabh Kataria, Palo Alto Research Center
Ani Nenkova, University of Pennsylvania
Kazi Hasan, IBM
Yang Song, Microsoft Research
Olena Medelyan, Entopix
Min-Yen Kan, National University of Singapore
Feifan Liu, Nuance Inc.
Niket Tandon, Max-Planck-Institut für Informatik
Preslav Nakov, Qatar Computing Research Institute
Fang Yuan, Institute for Infocomm Research, A*STAR
Pucktada Treeratpituk, Ministry Of Science and Technology, Thailand
Madian Khabsa, The Pennsylvania State University

Invited Speakers:

Min-Yen Kan, National University of Singapore
Preslav Nakov, Qatar Computing Research Institute

Table of Contents

Workshop Program

Thursday, July 30, 2015

9.10-9.30	Opening Remarks
9.30-10.30	*Keywords, Phrases, Clauses and Sentences: Topicality, Indicativeness and Informativeness at Scales* *Invited Talk by* Min-Yen Kan
10.30-11.00	Coffee Break
11.00-11.30	*Technical Term Extraction Using Measures of Neology* Christopher Norman and Akiko Aizawa
11.30-12.00	*Counting What Counts: Decompounding for Keyphrase Extraction* Nicolai Erbs, Pedro Bispo Santos, Torsten Zesch and Iryna Gurevych
12.00-14.00	Lunch
14.00-15.00	*The Web as an Implicit Training Set: Application to Noun Compounds Syntax and Semantics* *Invited Talk by* Preslav Nakov
15.00-15.30	*Reducing Over-generation Errors for Automatic Keyphrase Extraction using Integer Linear Programming* Florian Boudin
15.30-16.00	Coffee Break
16.00-16.30	*TwittDict: Extracting Social Oriented Keyphrase Semantics from Twitter* Suppawong Tuarob, Wanghuan Chu, Dong Chen and Conrad Tucker
16.30-17.00	*Identification and Classification of Emotional Key Phrases from Psychological Texts* Apurba Paul and Dipankar Das
17.00-17.30	Closing Remarks and Discussion

(Invited Talk) Keywords, Phrases, Clauses and Sentences: Topicality, Indicativeness and Informativeness at Scales

Min-Yen Kan
National University of Singapore
kanmy@comp.nus.edu.sg

About the Speaker:
Min-Yen Kan (BS;MS;PhD Columbia University) is an associate professor at the National University of Singapore. He is a senior member of the ACM and a member of the IEEE. Currently, he is an associate editor for the journal "Information Retrieval" and is the Editor for the ACL Anthology, the computational linguistics community's largest archive of published research. His research interests include digital libraries and applied natural language processing. Specific projects include work in the areas of scientific discourse analysis, full-text literature mining, machine translation and applied text summarization. More information about him and his group can be found at the WING homepage: http://wing.comp.nus.edu.sg/.

Proceedings of the ACL 2015 Workshop on Novel Computational Approaches to Keyphrase Extraction, page 1,
Beijing, China, July 30, 2015.

Technical Term Extraction Using Measures of Neology

Christopher Norman
Royal Institute of Technology
The University of Tokyo
chnor@kth.se

Akiko Aizawa
National Institute of Informatics
The University of Tokyo
aizawa@nii.ac.jp

Abstract

This study aims to show that frequency of occurrence over time for technical terms and keyphrases differs from general language terms in the sense that technical terms and keyphrases show a strong tendency to be recent coinage, and that this difference can be exploited for the automatic identification and extraction of technical terms and keyphrases. To this end, we propose two features extracted from temporally labelled datasets designed to capture surface level n-gram neology. Our analysis shows that these features, calculated over consecutive bigrams, are highly indicative of technical terms and keyphrases, which suggests that both technical terms and keyphrases are strongly biased to be surface level neologisms. Finally, we evaluate the proposed features on a gold-standard dataset for technical term extraction and show that the proposed features are comparable or superior to a number of features commonly used for technical term extraction.

1 Introduction

Keyphrases are terms assigned to documents, conventionally by its authors, that are intended chiefly as an aid in searching large collections of documents, as well as to give a brief overview of the document's contents. Technical terms are words or phrases that hold a specific meaning in specific domains or communities. Keyphrases are closely related to technical terms in the sense that the keyphrases assigned to a document are generally selected from the terminology of the document's domain. Keyphrases and technical terms show considerable conceptual overlap, and by extension, so do keyphrase and technical term extraction. As a consequence, these two are closely related research topics. In this study we will see technical term extraction and keyphrase extraction as distinct but related. We will take the view that the technical terms in a scientific article are likely candidates to be keyphrases for the document and consequently that technical term extraction methods might also be useful in keyphrase extraction.

We will show that features that capture the neology of term candidates can be used to extract technical terms, and that the basic assumptions that enable this extraction also hold true for keyphrases.

This paper is organized as follows: We first discuss how technical terms and keyphrases differ from general language terms in terms of neology. We then define features that capture this difference and analyze these features statistically using the SemEval-2010 dataset (Kim et al., 2010) and a gold-standard for technical term extraction derived from the same dataset (Chaimongkol and Aizawa, 2013). Our analysis shows that the proposed features reliably separate positive from negative examples, both of technical terms and of keyphrases. Furthermore, the histograms for the proposed features are very similar when calculated for technical terms and keyphrases, suggesting that technical terms and keyphrases have very similar neological properties. Finally, we demonstrate that this statistical bias can be used to reliably extract technical terms in a gold-standard dataset, and that the proposed features are comparable or superior to other features used in technical term extraction, with an F-score of 0.509 as compared to 0.593, 0.367, 0.361, and 0.204 for affix patterns, tf-idf, word shape, and POS tags respectively.

We argue that, given the high performance of the proposed features on technical term extraction, and given that we can show that the statistical properties that enable us to use them to extract technical terms also extend to keyphrases, the proposed features should also be useful in keyphrase extraction.

Proceedings of the ACL 2015 Workshop on Novel Computational Approaches to Keyphrase Extraction, pages 2–9, Beijing, China, July 30, 2015. ©2015 Association for Computational Linguistics

2 Related works

Most technical term extraction systems work fairly similarly to keyphrase extraction systems, using an initial n-gram or POS tag-based filtering to identify term candidates, then proceeding to narrow this list down using machine learning algorithms on various kinds of document statistics such as term frequency or the DICE coefficient (Justeson and Katz, 1995; Frantzi et al., 2000; Pinnis et al., 2012). For an in-depth summary of the state-of-the-art in technical term extraction, we refer to Vivaldi and Rodríguez (2007). For a summary of the state-of-the-art in keyphrase extraction, which largely follow the same pattern, we refer to Hasan and Ng (2014). The main difference in implementation might simply come down to a choice in top-level machine learning approach: in technical term extraction it makes sense to view the problem as a binary classification problem, whereas in keyphrase extraction it makes more sense to see the problem as a ranking problem.

Approaches based on frequency statistics extracted from the documents themselves are, however, not without their drawbacks. To begin with, for document statistics to be meaningful we will need a dataset that is large enough, consisting of documents that are large enough individually. We might also encounter problems if the documents are too large, because then the statistics might be drowned out by noise in the data (Hasan and Ng, 2014). We should also be careful about the topical composition of the data set – if the dataset only contains documents from a single domain, then we will have to approach the problem very differently than if the dataset contains documents from multiple domains. Preferably, we want methods that do not make these kinds of assumptions about the data set, methods that can be applied to documents of any size, and to document collections of any size or of any topical composition. In the best of worlds, we want methods that can be applied to document collections consisting of a single document, or even a single sentence.

One way to go beyond simple document statistics is to use external, pregenerated resources. To give some examples of this, Medelyan and Witten (2006) use a pregenerated domain thesaurus to conflate equivalent terms and to select candidates that are thematically related to each other, Hulth et al. (2006) use a pregenerated domain ontology to select candidates whose synonyms, hypernyms, and hyponyms also appear in the text, and Lopez and Romary (2010) use a terminology database as one way to measure the salience of term candidates for keyphrase extraction in scientific articles. Medelyan et al. (2009) use a somewhat more indirect external resource by taking the frequency by which a term candidate appears in Wikipedia links, divided by the frequency by which it appears in Wikipedia documents. The idea behind using external resources is that human annotators generally perform better than automatic systems, and resources produced by human beings are thus much more reliable than automatic methods, even if the resources themselves are only obliquely related to keyphrases.

However, depending on the speed by which the terminology of the subject field changes, any previously generated resource might become outdated very quickly. In a subject field such as law, where the terminology only changes imperceptibly over time (Lemmens, 2011), this is unlikely to be an issue, but in a quickly changing subject field such as information science, where the terminology has been reported to change by as much as 4% per year (Harris, 1979), it is likely that pregenerated resources will lag behind recent terminological developments. One selling point of the automatic extraction of keyphrases or technical terms is that automatic methods are able to respond to changes in the terminology of a subject field with the same speed that the terminology changes, but if we rely on pregenerated resources then we forsake this advantage, since these are unlikely to include terminology that only recently appeared in the subject field.

3 Theoretical basis

In this paper we will examine the use of external corpora in order to track the frequency of occurrence of n-grams over time, and use measures of neology as a way to extract technical terms. We are not aware of any previous attempts to use neology as a feature for technical term extraction, keyphrase extraction, or other kinds of natural language processing tasks. We will use the Google Ngrams dataset (Lin et al., 2012), where this information is already extracted. Although we use this dataset, mainly because of its convenience in our initial investigation, there is nothing keeping us from using other corpora consisting of raw documents, such as Pubmed. In particular, this would allow us to obtain more recent data than the Google Ngrams dataset, which only contains frequencies of occurrence from before 2008.

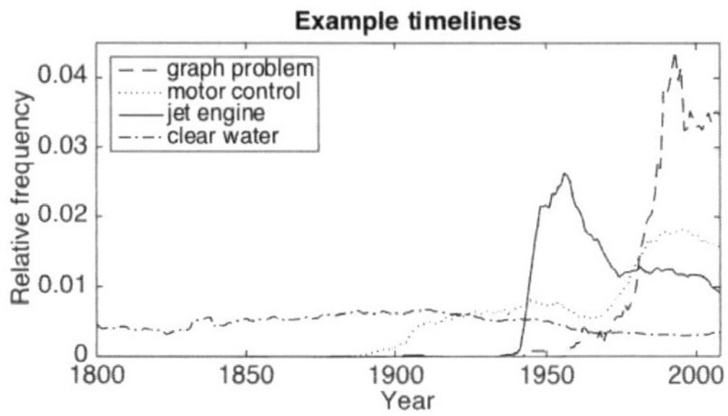

Figure 1: Example timelines (frequency of occurrence) for three technical terms and one non-technical term. The frequencies of occurrence for each timeline has been normalized to sum to one to fit all graphs in the same diagram.

In order to develop some intuition about how technical terms are adopted, let us look at the timelines for some technical terms in the Google Ngrams dataset (Figure 1). To begin with, all the technical terms (*graph problem*, *motor control*, and *jet engine*) are relatively recent coinage, and none of them were in use in the 19th century. In all three cases, there is some point in time at which the term gained momentum and began to surge in frequency. This characteristic is fairly typical of technical terms, although we can of course find general language terms that exhibit the same pattern of adoption. By contrast, the non-technical term (*clear water*) has been in use throughout the 19th and 20th century. Unlike technical terms, general language do not have generally observable characteristics, and the shape of the timelines vary greatly from case to case. The defining characteristic instead seems to be one of contrast: general language terms seldom have the steep curves that we can observe of the technical terms here.

We will formalize this difference and examine it statistically in the later parts of this study.

Of course, our ability to find neologisms by examining the frequency of occurrence of their surface forms necessitates that technical terms generally do not share surface forms with general language terms. If such is the case, then the general language senses of the terms are likely to drown out the technical term senses. For instance, consider a term like *worm* in computer security. The vast majority of the occurrences of the unigram *worm* in the Google Ngrams dataset are likely to be of the biological variety, and it is consequently impossible to tell from the Google Ngrams dataset alone that the computer security term only appeared in the later half of the 20th century[1]. Fortunately, the case where technical terms coincide with general language terms is rare, at least when considering terms composed of multiple words.

The overall recency of coinage of technical terms depends on the subject field – the majority of the terminology in e.g. computer science consists of terms whose surface forms were introduced no earlier than the middle of the 20th century, whereas subject fields such as mathematics and physics include terminology coined in the 19th century or earlier. Consequently, if we plot the frequency of usage of a neologism over time we would expect to see a curve similar to those in Figure 1, but we should expect that the curves may be shifted to the left or to the right, largely depending on the subject field.

Why are technical terms so often neologisms? It turns out that general language, which is what is ordinarily studied in linguistics, and special language, which is what we actually encounter in the documents commonly used for keyphrase extraction, differ quite substantially in linguistic aspects (Sager et al., 1980). One difference is that surface level neologisms are seldom created in general language. Rather, the creation of new surface forms generally occur in special language, from which the term might later be transferred to general language (Sager et al., 1980, p. 287). Consequently, terms that have appeared recently, given some specific point in time, are likely to be domain-specific at that point. The longer that has passed since the adoption of the term, the more likely it is that the term has been adopted into general language.

4 Measures of neology

We have noted that the shape of the timelines seem to indicate whether a given term is recent coinage, but in order to use these as input to machine learning algorithms, we need to distill the high dimensional data into low-dimensional features that retain the neological information.

[1] However, the term *computer worm* is a surface level neology. We might thus observe that new senses of the unigram *worm* appeared in the later half of the 19th century by examining bigrams.

What we want to extract is of course not necessarily the shape of the timelines, but whether the occurrences of the n-grams predominantly occur in the far right side on the time axis. In other words, we want to determine if the timeline is mainly concentrated on the right side. This is simple to do using statistical measures such as the mean and the standard deviation of the curves.

Let f_y^i denote the frequency of an n-gram i in year y. Then $p_i(y) = \frac{f_y^i}{\Sigma_y f_y^i}$ constitutes a probability density function, with the expected value:

$$\mu_i = \sum_y p_i(y) \cdot y = \frac{\sum_y f_y^i \cdot y}{\sum_y f_y^i}$$

How this "mean" should be interpreted might not be completely intuitively obvious, but for our purposes here it is enough to note that μ_i indicates where the curve is mainly concentrated. If the curve is concentrated around higher values of y then we have, by definition, a surface level neologism.

We can take the standard deviation of p_i in the same way:

$$\sigma_i^2 = \sum_y p_i(y) \cdot (y - \mu_i)^2 = \frac{\sum_y f_y^i \cdot (y - \mu_i)^2}{\sum_y f_y^i}$$

The standard deviation σ_i then yields a measure of how much the probability density is concentrated around μ_i, in other words, how "steep" the probability density is. A low standard deviation consequently indicates that the term has been adopted or abandoned rapidly. Low standard deviation should thus in general imply either surface level neologisms or fads. If we are only interested in how quickly a term has been adopted and not how quickly it might have been abandoned, then we can take a one-sided "standard deviation", by separating out the y for which $y < \mu_i$, but this does not seem to make much difference for the sake of the separability of technical terms. Those terms that have been adopted quickly also appear to be likely to quickly fall into relative disuse.

We should hasten to point out that there does not seem to exist any theoretical reasons to use the mean and standard deviation in this way. For instance, using the peak of the curve (i.e. the mode of the distribution) might have more intuitive appeal, since this should correspond to the point in time at which the term was in its most widespread use. However, the Google Ngrams dataset is often plagued by severe noise, in particular for less commonly used n-grams such as technical terms, and the peaks of the timelines are thus likely to be spurious. The mean and the standard deviation may be crude measures of shape, but they have the advantage of being robust against noise, and can generally be used with good results even for very noisy timelines.

Other intuitively appealing features, such as the first order derivatives of the timelines or the skewness of p_i have turned out not to be very useful, presumably because of the noise.

5 Statistical properties of technical terms and keyphrases

In this section, we examine statistically the features we propose, and show that both technical terms and keyphrases are strongly biased towards certain values for our features. We also underline the relationship between technical terms and keyphrases by showing that these are very similar in terms of neology.

To analyze keyphrases we will use the SemEval-2010 dataset (Kim et al., 2010), one of the most commonly used gold standards for keyphrase extraction. To analyze technical terms we will use a dataset consisting of the abstracts from the SemEval-2010 dataset manually annotated by two annotators such that all the technical term spans have been labeled (Chaimongkol and Aizawa, 2013). Since this dataset was constructed from the abstracts of the SemEval-2010 dataset we assume that these datasets are similar enough that analyzing and comparing the statistical properties of these two datasets is meaningful.

For the analysis in the following section, we construct three classes of data:

- We extract the n-grams that are part of the spans labeled as technical terms in the Chaimongkol-Aizawa dataset to obtain one set of positive examples of technical terms.
- We extract the constituent n-grams from the gold-standard keyphrases from the SemEval-2010 training dataset (using the combined set) to obtain one set of positive examples of keyphrases
- We extract the n-grams that are not part of the spans labeled as technical terms in the Chaimongkol-Aizawa dataset to obtain one

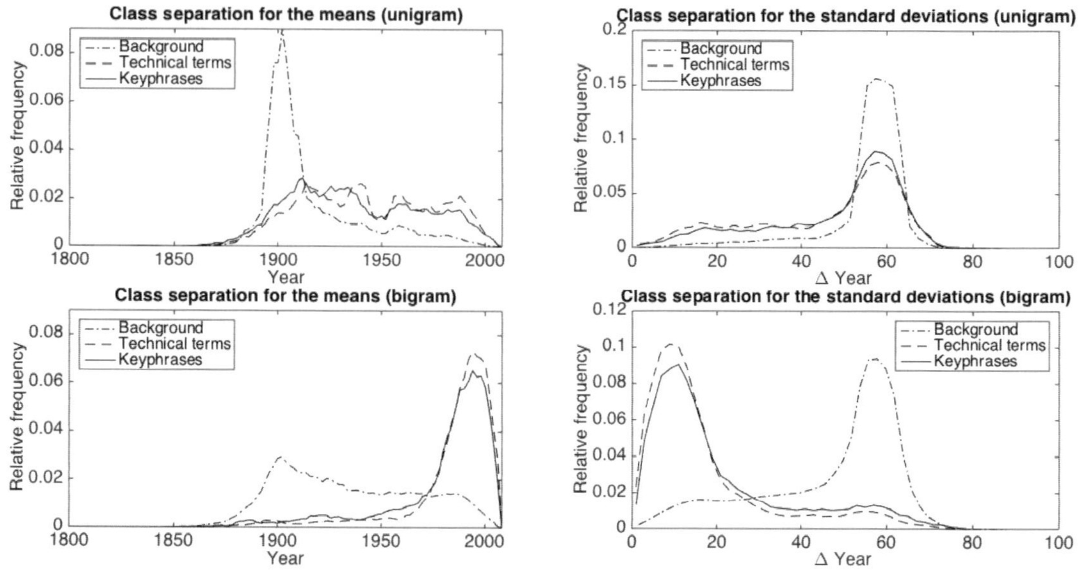

Figure 2: Class separation between technical terms, keyphrases, and background terms over μ_i (left) and σ_i (right), when considering unigrams (top), and bigrams (bottom). Histogram bin size was set to 2 in all cases. The resulting histograms have been smoothed using Matlab's default settings (moving average with span 5) and normalized to sum to one.

set of negative examples of both technical terms and keyphrases.

We could of course extract negative examples of keyphrases from the SemEval-2010 dataset, but it is not so clear that these would all unquestionably be negative examples of keyphrases. Given that inter-annotator agreement is generally very low for keyphrases, this set might well contain terms that could reasonably be considered keyphrases by other annotators. We here assume that the negative examples of technical terms also constitute negative examples of keyphrases, and that this set is less likely to contain borderline cases of keyphrases. Only using three classes of data also simplifies both the exposition and the processing.

For these three classes of n-grams, we extract the corresponding timelines from the Google Ngrams dataset over the period 1800–2008, and we calculate the means μ and standard deviations σ from these as defined in the preceding section. To analyze the features μ and σ we plot the histograms of the values for the technical term n-grams and the keyphrase n-grams versus the background n-grams (Figure 2).

In order for the features to be useful for either technical term extraction or keyphrase extraction we would like to see as little overlap as possible between the histograms of the positive and the negative examples. This seems to hold true for the bigrams, but not for the unigrams. In the unigram case we can see only a weak tendential difference in the histogram densities of the positive and negative examples.

We should point out that the mode of the histogram densities for the negative examples fall very close to the mean and standard deviation of a uniform distribution over the period 1800–2008. These would occur around 1904 and 60.48 respectively.

In all cases, the histograms for the technical terms and the keyphrases are very similar. This might not seem very surprising given that all the data is derived from the SemEval-2010 dataset, but it bears mentioning that these were annotated by different people, and more importantly, using very different annotation criteria.

We omit trigrams and higher order n-grams from consideration.

It is unlikely that higher order n-grams would help in keyphrase and technical term extraction, because the Google Ngrams dataset excludes any n-gram that has a total frequency of occurrence less than 50. This means that less frequently used

n-grams, such as technical terms, as well as higher order n-grams are likely to be missing (see Table 1). This problem is not very severe for unigrams and bigrams, but technical term trigrams suffer from data sparsity problem severe enough to essentially render them useless. Part of this problem might be due to the large mismatch between the dataset used for evaluation, and the Google Ngram dataset used to identify neology. If we were to use an external dataset from a more similar domain to the evaluation set, then we would expect to find a greater portion of the n-grams in the external dataset.

	Technical terms	Background
Unigram	97.5 %	100 %
Bigram	85.0 %	97.0 %
Trigram	25.5 %	71.0 %

Table 1: The ratio of n-gram in each class in the Chaimongkol-Aizawa dataset that occur in the Google Ngrams dataset. The percentages have been generated by chosing a random sample of 200 unigrams of each class, 200 bigrams of each etc., and checking if the n-gram occur in the Google Ngrams dataset using the web interface.

6 Evaluation on technical term extraction

In order to demonstrate that neology, as characterized by the features μ and σ, can be used to automatically extract technical terms, we implement a simple technical term extractor using these as features. We generally follow the approach taken by Chaimongkol and Aizawa (2013) and implement a conditional random field model to BIO-tag the dataset. The major difference in implementation is that we use the neology features extracted from Google Ngrams in the term extractor, and that we do not use features based on clustering.

For the sake of our CRF model, bigrams and unigrams are sufficient, since what we want to do is to obtain features corresponding to each node (i.e. to each unigram) and features corresponding to the links between the nodes (i.e. to each bigram). We might in theory achieve better performance with higher order n-grams, but in reality the results would be severely hampered by the sparsity problems for higher order n-grams.

Similarly to Chaimongkol and Aizawa, we implement a CRF model using the freely available state-of-the-art CRF framework CRFSuite[2], using five different feature sets:

1. POS TAGS using the Stanford POS tagger[3].
2. WORD SHAPE features extracted similarly to Chaimongkol and Aizawa. These include binary features such as whether the current token is capitalized, uppercased, or alphanumeric.
3. AFFIXES of length up to 4 characters extracted for all tokens. In other words, for the token *carbonization* we would extract *carb-*, *car-*, *ca-*, *c-*, *-tion*, *-ion*, *-on*, and *-n*.
4. TF-IDF for each unigram and bigram in the dataset.
5. NEOLOGY based features, in other words the mean and standard deviation of the Google Ngrams timeline as described in section 4.

The mutual information between each neighboring token in the dataset has also been tried, but this turned out to not have any perceptible effect on the results.

Because CRFSuite cannot handle continuous features, such as tf-idf, μ, or σ, we had to resort to discretizing these by binning. Appropriate bin sizes were established experimentally.

We apply the system on the labeled dataset where we attempt to binary classify each token into positive and negative examples, where positive examples are those that are part of a technical term compound, and negative those that are part of the background. We use the full dataset, and evaluate using 10-fold cross-validation.

Using all features, the system achieves an F-score around 0.7 for the technical term tokens, and an F-score around 0.9 for the non-technical term tokens.

To compare the different features with each other, we evaluate their performance individually (Table 2). The best performing feature turns out to be the affixes, although our neology features are quite comparable in performance. Neology performs better than all other features except affixes.

[2]http://www.chokkan.org/software/crfsuite/

[3]http://nlp.stanford.edu/software/tagger.shtml

	Technical terms			Non-technical terms		
	P	R	F_1	P	R	F_1
POS tags	**0.734**	0.118	0.204	0.835	**0.991**	0.906
Word shape	0.659	0.248	0.361	0.853	0.971	0.909
Affixes	0.673	**0.530**	**0.593**	**0.900**	0.943	**0.921**
tf-idf	0.600	0.244	0.367	0.852	0.964	0.904
Neology	0.637	0.423	0.509	0.881	0.947	0.913

Table 2: Term extractor performance in terms of correctly labeled tokens. Here, the system is only using a single feature class in each trial in order to compare the relative performance of each feature class.

	Technical terms			Non-technical terms		
	P	R	F_1	P	R	F_1
All features	0.728	0.673	0.700	0.929	0.944	0.936
– POS tags	0.728	0.656	0.690	0.925	0.946	0.935
– Word shape	0.719	0.671	0.694	0.928	0.942	0.935
– Affixes	**0.691**	**0.634**	**0.661**	**0.920**	**0.937**	**0.929**
– tf-idf	0.717	0.643	0.678	0.923	0.944	0.933
– Neology	0.715	0.647	0.679	0.923	0.943	0.933

Table 3: Term extractor performance in terms of correctly labeled tokens. Here, the system is using all but one feature class in each trial in order to compare the relative performance drop when each feature class is removed from the classifier.

It might be mentioned that these results are calculated over all tokens, even those where the neology features are missing because the corresponding n-grams do not occur in the Google Ngrams dataset. It is likely that the performance of the neology features would be higher if these were excluded from consideration. This might seem like cheating, but we should consider what would happen if we were to use another dataset with greater coverage, or some future improved version of the Google Ngrams dataset with greater coverage.

We also perform an ablation experiment to see how much the performance drops when excluding individual feature classes (Table 3). Similarly, the biggest drop occurs when excluding affixes. In this case, however, the differences between the different features are quite modest, which seems to imply that each single feature does not contain much information that is not also contained in the other features.

Compared to tf-idf, the neology feature is often able to correctly identify technical term spans containing terms which are also frequent in the remainder of the document collection, such as technical terms containing words like: *network*, *computer*, *function*, *algorithm*, *complexity*, *data*, *server*, *model*, or *vector*. It is much less easy to summarize where neology works well compared to the other features besides tf-idf.

Neology features are much less effective when the technical terms coincide with general language terms, for instance *worm*, *precision*, or *MAP*. This is generally only a problem in the unigram case, and bigrams such as *computer worm* or *average precision* generally do not have this problem.

7 Discussion

In this paper we have shown that technical terms tend to be recently coined, and that this statistical tendency is strong enough that it allows us to extract technical terms with reasonable accuracy. We have also shown that this statistical feature of technical terms also seem to hold true for keyphrases, and we therefore maintain that it is reasonable that similar features might also be useful in keyphrase extraction. We should not expect equally high performance in keyphrase extraction, however, since in keyphrase extraction we are not only interested in whether the output keyphrases are terms in the relevant domain, but also that they are significant in the document under consideration. What we do suggest is that neology can be useful for keyphrase extraction when used in concert with other features such as tf-idf that indicate significance or topicality.

The extraction of either technical terms or

keyphrases fundamentally depends upon the assumption that these are biased in certain ways. For instance, a common assumption taken in keyphrase extraction is that keyphrases are biased to occur more frequently at certain positions in the document. Another common assumption is that technical terms and keyphrases are biased to occur with different frequencies in certain communities, or that the contexts in which keyphrases and technical terms appear differ between different communities. Similarly to the position and community bias of keyphrases, we suggest that keyphrases also have a time bias, that the keyphrases of a document are skewed to be overrepresented in the contemporary and subsequent literature, but likely to be absent or severely underrepresented in the precedent literature.

The very high values of the means, and the very low values of the standard deviations observed for the technical terms in section 5 suggests that the majority of the technical term bigrams studied in this paper come from terms that only appeared after 1950. This might be explained by the fact that the datasets we use here are derived from the SemEval-2010 dataset, which is strongly biased towards computer science literature. It seems reasonable that the separation between the classes should generally be stronger in subject fields where the terminology tends to be very recent coinage than in fields with more mature terminology. If this is true, then the approach we propose here should work well for subject fields where the terminology is rapidly changing, and where the need for automatic extraction methods is arguably the greatest.

Acknowledgements

This work was supported by the Grant-in-Aid for Scientific Research (B) (15H02754) of the Japan Society for the Promotion of Science (JSPS).

References

Panot Chaimongkol and Akiko Aizawa. 2013. Utilizing LDA Clustering for Technical Term Extraction. *Proceedings of the Nineteenth Annual Meeting of the Association for Natural Language Processing, Nagoya*, pages 686–689.

Katerina Frantzi, Sophia Ananiadou, and Hideki Mima. 2000. Automatic recognition of multi-word terms: The C-value/NC-value method. *International Journal on Digital Libraries*, 3:115–130.

Jessica Harris. 1979. Terminology change: Effect on index vocabularies. *Information Processing & Management*, 15(2):77–88.

Kazi S. Hasan and Vincent Ng. 2014. Automatic Keyphrase Extraction : A Survey of the State of the Art. *Acl*, pages 1262–1273.

Anette Hulth, Jussi Karlgren, and Anna Jonsson. 2006. Automatic keyword extraction using domain knowledge. *Computational Linguistics and Intelligent Text Processing*, pages 472–482.

John S. Justeson and Slava M. Katz. 1995. Technical terminology: some linguistic properties and an algorithm for identification in text. *Natural Language Engineering*, 1:9–27.

Su Nam Kim, Olena Medelyan, Min-Yen Kan, and Timothy Baldwin. 2010. Semeval-2010 task 5: Automatic keyphrase extraction from scientific articles. *Proceedings of the 5th International Workshop on Semantic Evaluation*, pages 21–26.

Koen Lemmens. 2011. The slow dynamics of legal language: Festina lente? *Terminology*, 17:74–93.

Yuri Lin, Jean-baptiste Michel, Erez L. Aiden, Jon Orwant, Will Brockman, and Slav Petrov. 2012. Syntactic Annotations for the Google Books Ngram Corpus. *Proc. of the Annual Meeting of the Association for Computational Linguistics*, pages 169–174.

Patrice Lopez and Laurent Romary. 2010. HUMB : Automatic Key Term Extraction from Scientific Articles in GROBID. *Proceedings of the 5th International Workshop on Semantic Evaluation*, pages 248–251.

Olena. Medelyan and Ian H. Witten. 2006. Thesaurus based automatic keyphrase indexing. *Proceedings of the 6th ACM/IEEE-CS joint conference on Digital libraries*, pages 6–7.

Olena Medelyan, Eibe Frank, and Ian H. Witten. 2009. Human-competitive tagging using automatic keyphrase extraction. *Proceedings of the 2009 Conference on Empirical Methods in Natural Language Processing*, 3:1318–1327.

Mārcis Pinnis, Nikola Ljubešić, Dan Ştefănescu, Inguna Skadiņa, Marko Tadić, and Tatiana Gornostay. 2012. Term Extraction, Tagging, and Mapping Tools for Under-Resourced Languages. *Proceedings of the 10th Conference on Terminology and Knowledge Engineering*, pages 193–208.

Juan C. Sager, David Dungworth, and Peter F. McDonald. 1980. *English special languages: principles and practice in science and technology*. John Benjamins Publishing Company.

Jorge Vivaldi and Horacio Rodríguez. 2007. Evaluation of terms and term extraction systems: a practical approach. *Terminology*, 13:225–248.

Counting What Counts: Decompounding for Keyphrase Extraction

Nicolai Erbs[◇‡], Pedro Bispo Santos[◇], Torsten Zesch[§], Iryna Gurevych[◇‡]

◇ UKP Lab, Technische Universität Darmstadt
‡ UKP Lab, German Institute for Educational Research
§ Language Technology Lab, University of Duisburg-Essen
`http://www.ukp.tu-darmstadt.de`

Abstract

A core assumption of keyphrase extraction is that a concept is more important if it is mentioned more often in a document. Especially in languages like German that form large noun compounds, frequency counts might be misleading as concepts "hidden" in compounds are not counted. We hypothesize that using decompounding before counting term frequencies may lead to better keyphrase extraction. We identified two effects of decompounding: (i) enhanced frequency counts, and (ii) more keyphrase candidates. We created two German evaluation datasets to test our hypothesis and analyzed the effect of additional decompounding for keyphrase extraction.

1 Introduction

Most approaches for automatic extraction of keyphrases are based on the assumption that the more frequent a term or phrase is mentioned, the more important it is. Consequently, most extraction algorithms apply some kind of normalization, e.g. lemmatization or noun chunking (Hulth, 2003; Mihalcea and Tarau, 2004), in order to arrive with accurate counts. However, especially in Germanic languages the frequent use of noun compounds has an adverse effect on the reliability of frequency counts. Consider for example a German document that talks about *Lehrer* (Engl.: *teacher*) without ever mentioning the word "Lehrer" at all, because it is always part of compounds like *Deutschlehrer* (Engl.: *German teacher*) or *Gymnasiallehrer* (Engl.: *grammar school teacher*). Thus, we argue that the problem can be solved by splitting noun compounds in meaningful parts, i.e. by performing decompounding. Figure 1 give an example for decompounding

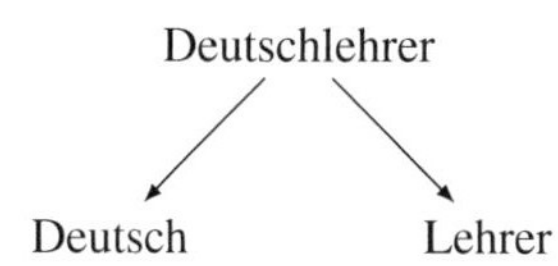

Figure 1: Decompounding of German term *Deutschlehrer* (Engl.: *German teacher*).

in German. The compound *Deutschlehrer* consists of the parts *Deutsch* (Engl.: *German*) and *Lehrer* (Engl.: *teacher*).

In this paper, we propose a comprehensive decompounding architecture and analyze the performance of four state-of-the-art algorithms. We then perform experiments on three German datasets, of which two have been created particularly for these experiments, in order to analyze the impact of decompounding on standard keyphrase extraction approaches. Decompounding has previously been successfully used in other applications, e.g. in machine translation (Koehn and Knight, 2003), information retrieval (Hollink et al., 2004; Alfonseca et al., 2008b; Alfonseca et al., 2008a), speech recognition (Ordelman, 2003), and word prediction (Baroni et al., 2002). Hasan and Ng (2014) have shown that infrequency errors are a major cause for lower keyphrase extraction results . To the best of our knowledge, we are the first to examine the influence of decompounding on keyphrase extraction.

2 Decompounding

Decompounding is usually performed in two steps: (i) a splitting algorithm creates candidates, and (ii) a ranking function decides which candidates are best suited for splitting the compound. For example, *Aktionsplan* has two splitting candidates: *Aktion(s)+plan* (Engl.: *action plan*) and *Akt+ion(s)+plan* (Engl.: *nude ion plan*).[1] After

[1] The additional 's' is a linking morpheme (Langer, 1998)

Proceedings of the ACL 2015 Workshop on Novel Computational Approaches to Keyphrase Extraction, pages 10–17,
Beijing, China, July 30, 2015. ©2015 Association for Computational Linguistics

generating the candidates, the ranking function assigns a score to each splitting candidate, including the original compound. We will now take a closer look on possible splitting algorithms and ranking functions.

2.1 Splitting algorithms

Left-to-Right grows a window over the input from left to right. When a word from a dictionary is found a split is generated. The algorithm is then applied recursively to the rest of the input.

JWord Splitter[2] performs a dictionary look-up from left to right, but continues this process if the remainder of the word is not right), it creates a split and stops. **Banana Splitter**[3] searches for the word from the right to the left, and if there is more than one possibility, the one with the longest split on the right side is taken as candidate. **Data Driven** counts the number of words in a dictionary, which contain a split at this position as prefix or suffix for every position in the input. A split is made at the position with the largest difference between prefix and suffix counts (Larson et al., 2000). **ASV Toolbox**[4] uses a trained Compact Patricia Tree to recursively split parts from the beginning and end of the word (Biemann et al., 2008). Unlike the other algorithms, it generates only a single split candidate at each recursive step. For that reason, it does not need a ranker. It is also the only supervised (using lists of existing compounds) approach tested.

2.2 Ranking functions

As stated earlier, the ranking functions are as important as the splitting algorithms, since a ranking function is responsible for assigning scores to each possible decompounding candidate. For the ranking functions, Alfonseca et al. (2008b) use a geometric mean of unigram frequencies (Equation 1), and a mutual information function (Equation 2).

$$r_{Freq}() \quad = \quad \left(\prod_{i}^{N} f(w_i) \right)^{\frac{1}{N}} \qquad (1)$$

$$r_{M.I.}() \quad = \quad \begin{cases} -f(c)\log f(c) & \text{if } N = 1 \\ \frac{1}{N-1}\sum_{i}^{N-1} \log \frac{bigr(w_i, w_{i+1})}{f(w_i)f(w_{i+1})} \end{cases} \qquad (2)$$

[2]github.com/danielnaber/jwordsplitter

[3]niels.drni.de/s9y/pages/bananasplit.html

[4]wortschatz.uni-leipzig.de/~cbiemann/software/toolbox/

Splitter	Ranker	P_{comp}	R_{comp}	P_{split}
Left-to-right	Freq.	.64	.58	.71
	M.I.	.26	.08	.33
JWord Splitter	Freq.	.67	.63	.79
	M.I.	.59	.20	.73
Banana Splitter	Freq.	.70	.40	.83
	M.I.	.66	.16	.81
Data Driven	Freq.	.49	.18	.70
	M.I.	.40	.04	.58
ASV ToolBox		**.80**	**.75**	**.87**

Table 1: Evaluation results of state-of-the-art decompounding systems.

In these equations, N is the number of fragments the candidate has, w is the fragment itself, $f(w)$ is the relative unigram frequency for that fragment w, $bigr(w_i, w_j)$ is the relative bigram frequency for the fragment w_i and w_j, c is the compound itself without being split.

2.3 Decompounding experiments

For evaluation, we use the corpus created by Marek (2006) as a gold standard to evaluate the performance of the decompounding methods. This corpus contains a list of 158,653 compounds, stating how each compound should be decompounded. The compounds were obtained from the issues 01/2000 to 13/2004 of the German computer magazine c't[5] in a semi-automatic approach. Human annotators reviewed the list to identify and correct possible errors. For calculating the required frequencies, we use the Web1T corpus[6] (Brants and Franz, 2006).

Koehn and Knight (2003) use a modified version of precision and recall for evaluating decompounding performance. Following Santos (2014), we decided to apply these metrics for measuring the splitting algorithms, and ranking the functions' performance. The following counts were used for evaluating the experiments on the compound level: *correct split (cs)*, a split fragment which was correctly identified and *wrong split (ws)*, a split fragment which was wrongly identified. P_{comp} and R_{comp} evaluate decompounding on the level of compounds, and we propose to use $P_{split} = \frac{\text{cs}}{\text{cs + ws}}$ to evaluate on the level of splits.

As we focus in this work on the influence of decompounding on improving the accuracy of fre-

[5]www.heise.de/ct/

[6]German version (see https://catalog.ldc.upenn.edu/LDC2009T25).

Dataset	peDOCS	MedForum	Pythag.
Number of doc.	2,644	102	60
∅ doc. length	14,016	135	277
Median doc. length	809	104	68
# keyphrases	30,051	853	622
∅ key / doc.	11.37	8.41	10 .37
∅ tokens / key	1.15	1.07	1.30
∅ characters / key	13.27	10.28	12 .22

Table 2: Corpus statistics of datasets.

quency counts, P_{split} is the best metric in our case. We can see in Table 1 that the ASV Toolbox splitting algorithm is the best performing system in respect to P_{split}. Thus, we select it as the decompounding algorithm in our keyphrase extraction experiments described in the next section.

3 Experiments

3.1 Datasets

For our evaluation, we could not rely on English datasets, as there is only very little compounding and thus the expected effect of decompounding is small. German is a good choice, as it is infamous for its heavy compounding, e.g. the well-known *Donaudampfschifffahrtskapitän* (Engl.: *captain of a steam ship on the river Danube*). For German keyphrase extraction, we can use the peDOCS datasets described in Erbs et al. (2013) and we created two additional datasets consisting of summaries of lesson transcripts (Pythagoras) and posts from a medical forum (MedForum). Table 2 summarizes their characteristics.

peDOCS consists of peer-reviewed articles, dissertations, and books from the educational domain published by researchers. The gold standard for this dataset was compiled by professional indexers and should thus be of high quality. We present two novel keyphrase datasets consisting of German texts. **MedForum** is composed of posts from a medical forum.[7] To our knowledge, it is the first dataset with keyphrase annotations from user-generated data in German. Two German annotators with university degrees identified a set of keyphrases for every document and following Nguyen and Kan (2007), the union of both sets are the final gold keyphrases. The **Pythagoras** dataset contains summaries of lesson transcripts compiled in the Pythagoras project.[8] Two annotators identified keyphrases after a training phase with discussion of three documents. As in the MedForum dataset, the gold standard consists of the union of lemmatized keyphrases by both annotators. All datasets contain a unranked list of keyphrases.

The peDOCS dataset is by far the largest of the sets, since it has been created over the course of several years. MedForum and Pythagoras contain fewer documents but each document is annotated by a fixed pair of human annotators. The average number of keyphrases is highest for peDOCS and lowest for MedForum. The length of the document also influences the number of keyphrases as short documents have fewer keyphrase candidates. Keyphrases in all three datasets are on average very short. The example in Figure 1 gives an example of a rather specific keyphrase which, however, consists of only one token. We believe that keyphrase extraction approaches benefit from decompounding more in cases of short documents. Longer documents provide more statistical data which reduces the need for additional statistical data obtained with decompounding.

3.2 Experimental Setup

For preprocessing, we rely on components from the DKPro Core framework (Eckart de Castilho and Gurevych, 2014) and on DKPro Lab (de Castilho and Gurevych, 2011) for building experimental pipelines. We use the Stanford Segmenter[9] for tokenization, TreeTagger (Schmid, 1994; Schmid, 1995) for lemmatization and part-of-speech tagging. Finally, we perform stopword removal and decompounding as described in Section 2. It should be noted that in most preprocessing pipelines, decompounding should be the last step, as it heavily influences POS-tagging. We extract all lemmas in the document as keyphrase candidates and rank them according to basic ranking approaches based on frequency counts and the position in the document. We do not use more sophisticated extraction approaches, as we want to examine the influence of decompounding as directly as possible. However, it has been shown that frequency-based heuristics are a very strong baseline (Zesch and Gurevych, 2009), and even supervised keyphrase extraction methods such as KEA (Witten et al., 1999) use term frequency and position as the most important features and will be

[7] www.medizin-forum.de/

[8] www.dipf.de/en/research/projects/pythagoras

[9] nlp.stanford.edu/software/segmenter.shtml

heavily influenced by decompounding.

We evaluate the following ranking methods: **tf-idf**$_{\text{constant}}$ ranks candidates according to their term frequency $f(t, d)$ in the document. **tf-idf** decreases the impact of words that occur in most documents. The term frequency count is normalized with the inverse document frequency in the test collection (Salton and Buckley, 1988).

$$\text{tf-idf} = f(t, d) \log \frac{|D|}{|d \in D : t \in d|} \quad (3)$$

In this formula $|D|$ is the number of documents and $|d \in D : t \in d|$ is the number of documents mentioning term t. As some document collections may be too small to allow computing reliable frequency estimates, we also evaluated **tf-idf**$_{web}$. Again, the document frequency is approximated by the frequency counts from the Web1T corpus. We take the **position** of a candidate as a baseline. The closer the keyword is to the beginning of the text, the higher it is ranked. This is not dependent on frequency counts, but decompounding can also have an influence if a compound that appears early in the document is split into parts that are now also possible keyphrase candidates. We test each of the ranking methods with (w) and without (w/o) decompounding.

3.3 Evaluation metrics

For the keyphrase experiments, we compare results in terms of precision and recall of the top-5 keyphrases (P@5), Mean Average Precision (MAP), and R-precision (R-p).[10] MAP is the average precision of extracted keyphrases from 1 to the number of extracted keyphrases, which can be much higher than ten. R-precision[11] is the ratio of true positives in the set of extracted keyphrases when as many keyphrases as there are gold keyphrases are extracted.[12]

4 Results and discussion

In order to assess the influence of decompounding on keyphrase extraction, we evaluate the selected extraction approaches with (w/) and without (w/o) decompounding. The final evaluation results will be influenced by two factors:

[10]Using the top-5 keyphrases reflects best the average number of keyphrases in our evaluation datasets and is common practice in related work (Kim et al., 2013).

[11]This is commonly in information retrieval and first used for keyphrase identification in Zesch and Gurevych (2009)

[12]Refer to Buckley and Voorhees (2000) for an overview of evaluation measures and their characteristics.

Method	Δ P@5	Δ R@5	Δ R-p.	Δ MAP
Position	.000	.000	.000	.000
tf-idf$_{\text{constant}}$	.039	.030	.022	.012
tf-idf	.031	.024	.025	.015
tf-idf$_{web}$	.035	.021	.024	.012

Table 3: Difference of results with decompounding on the MedForum dataset.

Enhanced frequency counts: As we have discussed before, the frequency counts will be more accurate, which should lead to higher quality keyphrases being extracted. This affects frequency-based rankings.

More keyphrase candidates: The number of keyphrase candidates might increase, as it is possible that some of the parts created by the decompounding were not mentioned in the document before. This is the special case of a enhanced frequency count going up from 0 to 1.

We perform experiments to investigate the influence of both effects, first, the enhanced frequency counts, and second, the newly introduced keyphrase candidates.

4.1 Enhanced frequency counts

In order to isolate the effect, we limit the list of keyphrase candidates to those that are already present in the document without decompounding. We selected the MedForum dataset for this analysis, because it contains many compounds and has the shortest documents which we believe is best suited for an additional decompounding step.

Table 3 shows improvements of evaluation results for keyphrase extraction approaches on the MedForum datasets. The improvement is measured as the difference of evaluation metrics of using extraction approaches with decompounding compared to not using any decompounding. This table does not show absolute numbers, instead it shows the increase of performance. Absolute values are not comparable to other experimental settings, because all gold keyphrases that do not appear in the text as lemmas are disregarded. We can thus analyze the effect of enhanced frequency counts in isolation. Results show that for tf-idf$_{\text{constant}}$, tf-idf, and tf-idf$_{web}$ our decompounding extension increases results on the MedForum dataset considering only candidates that are extracted without decompounding. Decompounding does not affect results for the position baseline as it is not based on frequency counting. For the frequency-based approaches, the effect is rather

Dataset	Decompounding w/o	w	Δ
peDOCS	.614	.632	.018
MedForum	.592	.631	.038
Pythagoras	.624	.625	.002

Table 4: Maximum recall for keyphrase extraction with and without decompounding for the datasets.

small in general, however consistent across all metrics and methods. The decompounding extension, however, has the effect of adding further keyphrase candidates.

4.2 More keyphrase candidates

The second effect of decompounding is that new terms are introduced that cannot be found in the original document. Table 4 shows the maximum recall for lemmas with and without decompounding on all German datasets. The maximum recall is obtained by assuming that given a list of candidates the best possible set of keyphrases are extracted. Keyphrase extraction with decompounding increases the maximum recall on all datasets by up to 3.8% points. It must be noted that the increase is due to more keyphrase candidates extracted, which increases the importance of the final ranking. The increase is higher for MedForum while it is lower for Pythagoras. Pythagoras comprises summaries of lesson transcripts for students in the ninth grade, thus teachers are less likely to use complex words which need to be decompounded. The smaller increase for peDOCS compared to MedForum is due to longer peDOCS documents. The longer a document is, the more likely a part in a compound also appears as an isolated token which limits the increase of maximum recall. peDOCS shows to have a higher maximum recall compared to collections with shorter documents because documents with more tokens also have more candidates. MedForum comprises forum data, which contains both medical terms and informal description of such terms. Furthermore, gold keyphrases were assigned to assist others in searching. This leads to having documents containing terms like *Augenschmerzen* (Engl.: *eye pain*) for which the gold keyphrase *Auge* (Engl.: *eye*) was assigned.

4.3 Combined results

Previously, we analyzed the effects of decompounding in isolation, now we analyze the combination of enhanced frequency counts and more keyphrase candidates on the overall results. Table 5 shows the complete results for the German datasets, described keyphrase extraction methods, and with and without decompounding.

For the peDOCS dataset, we see a negative effect of decompounding. Only the position baseline and tf-idf$_{\text{constant}}$ benefit from decompounding in terms of mean average precision (MAP), while they yield lower results in terms of the other evaluation metrics. The improvement of the position baseline in terms of MAP might be to several correctly extracted keyphrases beyond the top-5 extracted keyphrases. We have previously discussed that peDOCS has on average the longest documents and most likely contains all gold keyphrases multiple times in the document text. For this reason, frequency-based approaches do not benefit from additional frequency information obtained from compounds. Many compounds are composed of common words, which already appear in the document. On the contrary, more common keyphrases are weighted higher, which hurts results in the case of peDOCS with highly-specialized and longer keyphrases. Depending on the task, this might be an undesired behavior.[13]

The only dataset for which the decompounding yields higher results is the MedForum dataset. Results improve with decompounding for tf-idf$_{\text{constant}}$ and tf-idf. As can be seen in Table 4, enhanced frequency counts improve results, and yield a higher maximum recall. Contrary to the other tf-idf configurations, results for tf-idf$_{web}$ decrease with decompounding. This leads to the observation that, besides the effect of enhanced ranking and more keyphrase candidates, a third effect influences results of keyphrase extraction methods: The ranking of additional keyphrase candidates obtained from decompounding. These candidates might appear infrequently in isolation and are ranked high if external document frequencies (*df* values) are used. Compound parts which do not appear in isolation[14]—hence, no good keyphrases—are ranked high in case of tf-idf$_{web}$ because their document frequency from the web is very low. In case of classic tf-idf they are ranked low because they are normalized with doc-

[13]When searching for documents, highly-specialized keyphrases might be better suited, while common keyphrases might be better suited for clustering of documents.

[14]The verb *begießen* (Engl.: *to water*) can be split into the verb *gießen* (Engl.: *to pour*) and the prefix *be* which does not appear as an isolated word.

		Decompounding											
		Precision@5			Recall@5			R-precision			MAP		
Dataset	Method	w/o	w/	Δ	w/o	w/	Δ	w/o	w/	Δ	w/o	w/	Δ
peDOCS	*Upper bound*	.856	.864	.012	.393	.403	.010	.614	.632	.018	.614	.632	.018
	Position	.096	.068	-.028	.042	.030	-.012	.092	.080	-.012	.083	.086	.003
	tf-idf$_{constant}$	.170	.160	-.010	.075	.070	-.004	.127	.125	-.002	.123	.123	.001
	tf-idf	.137	.117	-.020	.060	.051	-.009	.107	.088	-.019	.112	.099	-.014
	tf-idf$_{web}$	**.188**	.168	-.020	**.083**	.074	-.009	**.139**	.126	-.013	**.139**	.129	-.010
MedForum	*Upper bound*	.867	.890	.023	.397	.422	.025	.592	.631	.038	.592	.631	.038
	Position	.082	.073	-.010	.049	.043	-.006	.101	.090	-.011	.142	.130	-.012
	tf-idf$_{constant}$	.149	.161	.012	.089	.096	.007	.144	.145	.001	.165	.162	-.003
	tf-idf	.235	**.282**	.047	.140	**.168**	.028	.210	**.234**	.025	.203	**.210**	.007
	tf-idf$_{web}$	.231	.165	-.067	.138	.098	-.040	.223	.159	-.064	.206	.180	-.027
Pythagoras	*Upper bound*	.941	.942	.001	.344	.344	.001	.624	.625	.002	.624	.625	.002
	Position	.030	.023	-.007	.014	.011	-.003	.044	.022	-.022	.106	.075	-.031
	tf-idf$_{constant}$	.137	.087	-.050	.066	.042	-.024	.143	.103	-.040	.153	.121	-.032
	tf-idf	.150	.150	.000	.072	.072	.000	.113	.114	.001	.141	.136	-.005
	tf-idf$_{web}$	**.187**	.100	-.087	**.090**	.048	-.042	**.205**	.102	-.103	**.191**	.136	-.055

Table 5: Results for keyphrase extraction approaches without (w/o) and with (w/) decompounding.

ument frequencies from a corpus where decompounding has been applied. In case of tf-idf$_{web}$, no decompounding has been applied. The effect of the poor ranking of newly introduced keyphrase candidates needs to be investigated further by conducting a manual analysis of the decompounding performance and the creation of non-words.

For the Pythagoras dataset, keyphrase extraction approaches yield similar results as for peDOCS. Decompounding decreases results, only results for tf-idf stay stable. As seen earlier (see Table 4), decompounding does not raise the maximum recall much (only by .002). As before in the case of the MedForum dataset, tf-idf$_{web}$ is influenced negatively by the decompounding extension. Results for tf-idf$_{web}$ decrease by .103 in terms of R-precision, which is a reduction of more than 50%. The ranking of keyphrases is hurt by many keyphrases, which appear as parts of compounds. They are ranked high because they infrequently appear as separate words. Considering the characteristics of keyphrases in Pythagoras, we see that keyphrases are rather long with 12.22 characters per keyphrase. This leads to the observation that the style of the keyphrases has an effect on the applicability of decompounding. Datasets with more specific keyphrases are less likely to benefit from decompounding.

5 Conclusions and future work

We presented a decompounding extension for keyphrase extraction. We created two new datasets to analyze these effects and showed that decompounding has the potential to increase results for keyphrase extraction on shorter German documents. We identified two effects of decompounding relevant for keyphrase extraction: (i) enhanced frequency counts, and (ii) more keyphrase candidates. We find that the first effect slightly increases results when updating the term frequencies, while including the second effect in the evaluation, reduces results for two of three datasets. We thus conclude that the effect of decompounding for keyphrases extraction requires further analysis, but may be a useful feature for supervised systems (Berend and Farkas, 2010).

In the future, we propose to further analyze characteristics of good keyphrases and whether they often are compounds. We see the potential for better decompounding approaches as any improvements on this task may have positive effects on keyphrase extraction. We would also like to investigate other effects that make tasks like keyphrase extraction especially hard. Named entity disambiguation might improve results further as some concepts are mentioned frequently in a text but always with another surface form. We make our experimental framework available to the community to foster future research.

Acknowledgments

This work has been supported by the Volkswagen Foundation as part of the Lichtenberg-Professorship Program under grant No. I/82806, by the Klaus Tschira Foundation under project No. 00.133.2008, and by the German Institute for Educational Research (DIPF) We thank the anonymous reviewers for their helpful comments.

References

Enrique Alfonseca, Slaven Bilac, and Stefan Pharies. 2008a. Decompounding Query Keywords from Compounding Languages. In *Proceedings of the 46th Annual Meeting of the Association for Computational Linguistics on Human Language Technologies: Short Papers*, HLT-Short '08, pages 253–256, Stroudsburg, PA, USA. Association for Computational Linguistics.

Enrique Alfonseca, Slaven Bilac, and Stefan Pharies. 2008b. German Decompounding in a Difficult Corpus. In *Computational Linguistics and Intelligent Text Processing*, volume 4919 of *Lecture Notes in Computer Science*, pages 128–139. Springer Berlin Heidelberg.

Marco Baroni, Johannes Matiasek, and H Trost. 2002. Predicting the Components of German Nominal Compounds. *ECAI*, pages 1–12.

Gábor Berend and Richárd Farkas. 2010. SZTERGAK: Feature Engineering for Keyphrase Extraction. In *Proceedings of the 5th International Workshop on Semantic Evaluation*, SemEval '10, pages 186–189, Stroudsburg, PA, USA.

Chris Biemann, Uwe Quasthoff, Gerhard Heyer, and Florian Holz. 2008. ASV Toolbox: a Modular Collection of Language Exploration Tools. In *Proceedings of the Sixth International Conference on Language Resources and Evaluation (LREC'08)*, pages 1760–1767, Paris. European Language Resources Association (ELRA).

Thorsten Brants and Alex Franz. 2006. Web 1T 5-Gram Version 1. In *Linguistic Data Consortium*, Philadelphia.

Chris Buckley and Ellen M. Voorhees. 2000. Evaluating Evaluation Measure Stability. In *Proceedings of the 23rd Annual International ACM SIGIR Conference on Research and Development in Information Retrieval - SIGIR '00*, pages 33–40, New York, New York, USA.

Richard Eckart de Castilho and Iryna Gurevych. 2011. A Lightweight Framework for Reproducible Parameter Sweeping in Information Retrieval. In *Proceedings of the 2011 Workshop on Data Infrastructures for Supporting Information Retrieval Evaluation*, DESIRE '11, pages 7–10, New York, NY, USA. ACM.

Richard Eckart de Castilho and Iryna Gurevych. 2014. A Broad-coverage Collection of Portable NLP Components for Building Shareable Analysis Pipelines. In *Proceedings of the Workshop on Open Infrastructures and Analysis Frameworks for HLT at COLING 2014*, pages 1–11.

Nicolai Erbs, Iryna Gurevych, and Marc Rittberger. 2013. Bringing Order to Digital Libraries: From Keyphrase Extraction to Index Term Assignment. *D-Lib Magazine*, 19(9/10):1–16.

Kazi Saidul Hasan and Vincent Ng. 2014. Automatic keyphrase extraction: A survey of the state of the art. *Proceedings of the Association for Computational Linguistics (ACL), Baltimore, Maryland: Association for Computational Linguistics.*

Vera Hollink, Jaap Kamps, Christof Monz, and Maarten de Rijke. 2004. Monolingual Document Retrieval for European Languages. *Information Retrieval*, 7(1/2):33–52.

Anette Hulth. 2003. Improved Automatic Keyword Extraction given more Linguistic Knowledge. In *Proceedings of the Conference on Empirical Methods in Natural Language Processing*, pages 216–223.

Su Nam Kim, Olena Medelyan, Min-Yen Kan, and Timothy Baldwin. 2013. Automatic Keyphrase Extraction from Scientific Articles. *Language Resources and Evaluation*, 47:723–742.

Philipp Koehn and Kevin Knight. 2003. Empirical Methods for Compound Splitting. In *Proceedings of the Tenth Conference on European Chapter of the Association for Computational Linguistics - Volume 1*, EACL '03, pages 187–193, Stroudsburg, PA, USA. Association for Computational Linguistics.

Stefan Langer. 1998. Zur Morphologie und Semantik von Nominalkomposita. In *Tagungsband der 4. Konferenz zur Verarbeitung natürlicher Sprache (KONVENS)*, pages 83–97.

Martha Larson, Daniel Willett, Joachim Koehler, and Gerhard Rigoll. 2000. Compound Splitting and Lexical Unit Recombination for Improved Performance of a Speech Recognition System for German Parliamentary Speeches. In *Proceedings of the 6th International Conference on Spoken Language Processing (ICSLP)*, pages 945–948.

Torsten Marek. 2006. Analysis of German Compounds using Weighted Finite State Transducers. *Bachelor thesis, University of Tübingen.*

Rada Mihalcea and Paul Tarau. 2004. TextRank: Bringing Order into Texts. In *Proceedings of Empirical Methods for Natural Language Processing*, pages 404–411.

Thuy Dung Nguyen and Min-Yen Kan. 2007. Keyphrase Extraction in Scientific Publications. In *Proceedings of International Conference on Asian Digital Libraries*, volume 4822 of *Lecture Notes in Computer Science*, pages 317–326.

R. J. F. Ordelman. 2003. *Dutch Speech Recognition in Multimedia Information Retrieval.* Ph.D. thesis, University of Twente, Enschede, Enschede, October.

Gerard Salton and Christopher Buckley. 1988. Term-Weighting Approaches in Automatic Text Retrieval. *Information Processing & Management*, 24(5):513–523.

Pedro Bispo Santos. 2014. Using compound lists for german decompounding in a back-off scenario. In *Workshop on Computational, Cognitive, and Linguistic Approaches to the Analysis of Complex Words and Collocations (CCLCC 2014)*, pages 51–55.

Helmut Schmid. 1994. Probabilistic Part-of-Speech Tagging Using Decision Trees. In *International Conference on New Methods in Language Processing*, pages 44–49, Manchester, UK.

Helmut Schmid. 1995. Improvements in Part-of-Speech Tagging with an Application to German. In *Proceedings of the ACL SIGDAT-Workshop*, volume 21, pages 1–9.

Ian H Witten, Gordon W Paynter, and Eibe Frank. 1999. KEA: Practical Automatic Keyphrase Extraction. In *Proceedings of the 4th ACM Conference on Digital Libraries*, pages 254–255.

Torsten Zesch and Iryna Gurevych. 2009. Approximate Matching for Evaluating Keyphrase Extraction. In *Proceedings of the 7th International Conference on Recent Advances in Natural Language Processing*, pages 484–489.

(Invited Talk) The Web as an Implicit Training Set: Application to Noun Compounds Syntax and Semantics

Preslav Nakov
Qatar Computing Research Institute
pnakov@qf.org.qa

Abstract

The 60-year-old dream of computational linguistics is to make computers capable of communicating with humans in natural language. This has proven hard, and thus research has focused on sub-problems. Even so, the field was stuck with manual rules until the early 90s, when computers became powerful enough to enable the rise of statistical approaches. Eventually, this shifted the main research attention to machine learning from text corpora, thus triggering a revolution in the field.

Today, the Web is the biggest available corpus, providing access to quadrillions of words; and, in corpus-based natural language processing, size does matter. Unfortunately, while there has been substantial research on the Web as a corpus, it has typically been restricted to using page hit counts as an estimate for n-gram word frequencies; this has led some researchers to conclude that the Web should be only used as a baseline.

In this talk, I will reveal some of the hidden potential of the Web that lies beyond the n-gram, with focus on the syntax and semantics of English noun compounds. First, I will present a highly accurate lightly supervised approach based on surface markers and linguistically-motivated paraphrases that yields state-of-the-art results for noun compound bracketing: e.g., "[[liver cell] antibody]" is left-bracketed, while "[liver [cell line]]" is right-bracketed. Second, I will present a simple unsupervised method for mining implicit predicates that can characterize the semantic relations holding between the nouns in noun compounds, e.g., "malaria mosquito" is a "mosquito that carries/spreads/causes/transmits/brings/infects with/... malaria". Finally, I will show how these ideas can be used to improve statistical machine translation.

About the Speaker:
Preslav Nakov is a Senior Scientist at the Qatar Computing Research Institute (QCRI). He received his Ph.D. in Computer Science from the University of California at Berkeley in 2007 (supported by a Fulbright grant and a UC Berkeley fellowship). Before joining QCRI, Preslav was a Research Fellow at the National University of Singapore. He has also spent a few months at the Bulgarian Academy of Sciences and the Sofia University, where he was an honorary lecturer. Preslav's research interests include lexical semantics (in particular, multi-word expressions, noun compounds syntax and semantics, and semantic relation extraction), machine translation, Web as a corpus, and biomedical text processing.

Preslav was involved in many activities related to lexical semantics. He is a member of the SIGLEX board, he is co-chairing SemEval'2014, SemEval'2015, and SemEval'2016, and he has co-organized several SemEval tasks, e.g., on the semantics of noun compounds, on semantic relation extraction, on sentiment analysis on Twitter, and on community question answering. He has co-chaired MWE in 2009 and 2010, as well as other semantics workshops such as RELMS, and he was an area chair of *SEM'2013. He was also a guest co-editor for the 2013 special issue of the journal of Natural Language Engineering on the syntax and semantics of noun compounds, and he is currently a guest co-editor of a special issue of LRE on SemEval-2014 and Beyond. In 2013, he has published a Morgan & Claypool book on semantic relation extraction; he has given a tutorial on the same topic at RANLP'2013, and he is giving a similar one at EMNLP'2015.

Proceedings of the ACL 2015 Workshop on Novel Computational Approaches to Keyphrase Extraction, page 18,
Beijing, China, July 30, 2015.

Reducing Over-generation Errors for Automatic Keyphrase Extraction using Integer Linear Programming

Florian Boudin
LINA - UMR CNRS 6241, Université de Nantes, France
florian.boudin@univ-nantes.fr

Abstract

We introduce a global inference model for keyphrase extraction that reduces over-generation errors by weighting sets of keyphrase candidates according to their component words. Our model can be applied on top of any supervised or unsupervised word weighting function. Experimental results show a substantial improvement over commonly used word-based ranking approaches.

1 Introduction

Keyphrases are words or phrases that capture the main topics discussed in a document. Automatically extracted keyphrases have been found to be useful for many natural language processing and information retrieval tasks, such as summarization (Litvak and Last, 2008), opinion mining (Berend, 2011) or text categorization (Hulth and Megyesi, 2006). Despite considerable research effort, the automatic extraction of keyphrases that match those of human experts remains challenging (Kim et al., 2010).

Recent work has shown that most errors made by state-of-the-art keyphrase extraction systems are due to over-generation (Hasan and Ng, 2014). Over-generation errors occur when a system correctly outputs a keyphrase because it contains an important word, but at the same time erroneously predicts other keyphrase candidates as keyphrases because they contain the same word. One reason these errors are frequent is that many unsupervised systems rank candidates according to the weights of their component words, e.g. (Wan and Xiao, 2008a; Liu et al., 2009), and many supervised systems use unigrams as features, e.g. (Turney, 2000; Nguyen and Luong, 2010).

While weighting words instead of phrases may seem rather blunt, it offers several advantages. In practice, words are usually much easier to extract, match and weight, especially for short documents where many phrases may not be statistically frequent (Liu et al., 2011).

Selecting keyphrase candidates according to their component words may also turn out to be useful for reducing over-generation errors if one can ensure that the importance of each word is counted only once in the set of extracted keyphrases. To do so, keyphrases should be extracted as a set rather than independently. Finding the optimal set of keyphrases is a combinatorial optimisation problem, and can be formulated as an integer linear program (ILP) which can be solved exactly using off-the-shelf solvers.

In this work, we propose an ILP formulation for keyphrase extraction that can be applied on top of any word weighting scheme. Through experiments carried out on the SemEval dataset (Kim et al., 2010), we show that our model increases the performance of both supervised and unsupervised word weighting keyphrase extraction methods.

The rest of this paper is organized as follows. In Section 2, we describe our ILP model for keyphrase extraction. Our experiments are presented in Section 3. In Section 4, we briefly review the previous work, and we conclude in Section 5.

2 Method

Our global inference model for keyphrase extraction consists of three steps. First, keyphrase candidates are extracted from the document using heuristic rules. Second, words are weighted using either supervised or unsupervised methods. Third, finding the optimal subset of keyphrase candidates is cast as an ILP and solved using an off-the-shelf solver.

2.1 Keyphrase candidate selection

Candidate selection is the task of identifying the words or phrases that have properties similar to

Proceedings of the ACL 2015 Workshop on Novel Computational Approaches to Keyphrase Extraction, pages 19–24,
Beijing, China, July 30, 2015.

those of manually assigned keyphrases. First, we apply the following pre-processing steps to the document: sentence segmentation[1], word tokenization[2] and Part-Of-Speech (POS) tagging[3].

Following previous work (Wan and Xiao, 2008a; Bougouin et al., 2013), we use the sequences of nouns and adjectives as keyphrase candidates. Candidates that have less than three characters, that contain only adjectives, or that contain stop-words[4] are filtered out. These heuristic rules are designed to avoid spurious instances and keep the number of candidates to a minimum (Hasan and Ng, 2014). All words are stemmed using Porter's stemmer (Porter, 1980).

2.2 Word weighting functions

The performance of our model depends on how word weights are estimated. Here, we experiment with three methods for assigning importance weights to words. The first two are unsupervised weighting functions, namely TF×IDF (Spärck Jones, 1972) and TextRank (Mihalcea and Tarau, 2004), which have been extensively used in prior work (Hasan and Ng, 2010). We also apply a supervised model for predicting word importance based on (Hong and Nenkova, 2014).

2.2.1 TF×IDF

The weight of each word t is estimated using its frequency $tf(t, d)$ in the document d and how many other documents include t (inverse document frequency), and is defined as:

$$\text{TF} \times \text{IDF}(t, d) = tf(t, d) \times log(D/D_t)$$

where D is the total number of documents and D_t is the number of documents containing t.

2.2.2 TextRank

A co-occurrence graph is first built from the document in which nodes are words and edges represent the number of times two words co-occur in the same sentence. TextRank (Mihalcea and Tarau, 2004), a graph-based ranking algorithm, is then used to compute the importance weight of each word. Let d be a damping factor[5], the TextRank score $S(V_i)$ of a node V_i is initialized to a default value and computed iteratively until convergence using the following equation:

$$S(V_i) = (1 - d) + \left(d \times \sum_{V_j \in \mathcal{N}(V_i)} \frac{w_{ji} \times S(V_j)}{\sum_{V_k \in \mathcal{N}(V_j)} w_{jk}} \right)$$

where $\mathcal{N}(V_i)$ is the set of nodes connected to V_i and w_{ji} is the weight of the edge between nodes V_j and V_i.

TextRank implements the concept of "voting", i.e. a word is important if it is highly connected to other words and if it is connected to important words.

2.2.3 Logistic regression

We train a logistic regression model[6] for assigning importance weights to words in the document based on (Hong and Nenkova, 2014). Reference keyphrases in the training data are used to generate positive and negative examples. For a word in the document (restricted to adjectives and nouns), we assign label 1 if the word appears in the corresponding reference keyphrases, otherwise we assign 0. We use the relative position of the first occurrence, the presence in the first sentence and the TF×IDF weight as features. These features have been extensively used in supervised keyphrase extraction approaches, and have been shown to perform consistently well (Hasan and Ng, 2014).

2.3 ILP model definition

Our model is an adaptation of the concept-based ILP model for summarization introduced by (Gillick and Favre, 2009), in which sentence selection is cast as an instance of the budgeted maximum coverage problem[7]. The key assumption of our model is that the value of a set of keyphrase candidates is defined as the sum of the weights of the unique words it contains. That way, a set of candidates only benefits from including each word once. Words are thus assumed to be independent, that is, the value of including a word is not affected by the presence of any other word in the set of keyphrases.

Formally, let w_i be the weight of word i, x_i and c_j two binary variables indicating the pres-

[1] We use Punkt Sentence Tokenizer from NLTK.

[2] We use Penn Treebank Tokenizer from NLTK.

[3] We use the Stanford Part-Of-Speech Tagger (Toutanova et al., 2003).

[4] We use the english stop-list from NLTK.

[5] We set d to 0.85 as in (Mihalcea and Tarau, 2004).

[6] We use the Logistic Regression classifier from scikit-learn with default parameters.

[7] Given a collection S of sets with associated costs and a budget L, find a subset $S' \subseteq S$ such that the total cost of sets in S' does not exceed L, and the total weight of elements covered by S' is maximized (Khuller et al., 1999).

ence of word i and candidate j in the set of extracted keyphrases, Occ_{ij} an indicator of the occurrence of word i in candidate j and N the maximum number of extracted keyphrases, our model is described as:

$$\max \quad \sum_i w_i x_i \tag{1}$$
$$s.t. \quad \sum_j c_j \leq N \tag{2}$$
$$c_j Occ_{ij} \leq x_i, \quad \forall i, j \tag{3}$$
$$\sum_j c_j Occ_{ij} \geq x_i, \quad \forall i \tag{4}$$
$$x_i \in \{0, 1\} \quad \forall i$$
$$c_j \in \{0, 1\} \quad \forall j$$

The constraints formalized in equations 3 and 4 ensure the consistency of the solution: selecting a candidate leads to the selection of all the words it contains, and selecting a word is only possible if it is present in at least one selected candidate.

By summing over word weights, this model overly favors long candidates. Indeed, given two keyphrase candidates, one being included in the other (e.g. *uddi registries* and *multiple uddi registries*), this model always selects the longest one as its contribution to the objective function is larger. To correct this bias, a regularization term is added to the objective function:

$$\max \quad \sum_i w_i x_i - \lambda \sum_j \frac{(l_j - 1)c_j}{1 + substr_j} \tag{5}$$

where l_j is the size, in words, of candidate j, and $substr_j$ the number of times c_j occurs as a subtring in the other candidates. This regularization penalizes the candidates that are composed of more than two words, and is dampened for candidates that occur frequently as substrings in other candidates. Here, we assume that for multiple candidates of the same size, the one that is less frequent in the document should be stressed first.

The resulting ILP is then solved exactly using an off-the-shelf solver[8]. The solving process takes less than a second per document on average. The N candidate keyphrases returned by the solver are selected as keyphrases.

[8]We use GLPK, `http://www.gnu.org/software/glpk/`

3 Experiments

3.1 Experimental settings

We carry out our experiments on the SemEval dataset (Kim et al., 2010), which is composed of scientific articles collected from the ACM Digital Library. The dataset is divided into training (144 documents) and test (100 documents) sets. We use the set of combined author- and reader-assigned keyphrases as reference keyphrases.

We follow the common practice (Kim et al., 2010) and evaluate the performance of our method in terms of precision (P), recall (R) and f-measure (F) at the top N keyphrases[9]. Extracted and reference keyphrases are stemmed to reduce the number of mismatches.

For each word weighting function, namely TF×IDF, TextRank and Logistic regression, we compare the performance of our ILP model (hereafter `ilp`) with that of two word-based weighting baselines. The first baseline (hereafter `sum`) simply ranks keyphrase candidates according to the sum of the weights of their component words as in (Wan and Xiao, 2008b; Wan and Xiao, 2008a). The second baseline (hereafter `norm`) consists in scoring keyphrase candidates by computing the sum of the weights of their component words normalized by their length as in (Boudin, 2013).

As a post-processing step, we remove redundant keyphrases from the ranked lists generated by both baselines. A keyphrase is considered redundant if it is included in another keyphrase that is ranked higher in the list.

IDF weights are computed on the training set. The regularization parameter λ is set, for all the experiments, to the value that achieves the best performance on the training set, that is 0.3 for TF×IDF, 0.4 for TextRank and 1.2 for Logistic regression.

3.2 Results

The performance of our model on top of different word weighting functions is shown in Table 1. Overall, our model consistently improves the performance over the baselines. We observe that the results for `sum` are very low. Summing the word weights favors long candidates and is prone to over-generation errors, as illustrated by the example in Table 2.

[9]Scores are computed using the evaluation script provided by the SemEval organizers.

Weighting + Ranking	Top-5 candidates P	R	F	Top-10 candidates P	R	F
TF×IDF + `sum`	5.6	1.9	2.8	5.3	3.5	4.2
+ `norm`	19.2	6.7	9.9	15.1	10.6	12.3
+ `ilp`	25.4	9.1	13.3†	17.5	12.4	14.4†
TextRank + `sum`	4.5	1.6	2.3	4.0	2.8	3.3
+ `norm`	18.8	6.6	9.6	14.5	10.1	11.8
+ `ilp`	22.6	8.0	11.7†	17.4	12.2	14.2†
Logistic regression + `sum`	4.2	1.5	2.2	4.7	3.4	3.9
+ `norm`	23.8	8.3	12.2	18.9	13.3	15.5
+ `ilp`	29.4	10.4	15.3†	19.8	14.1	16.3

Table 1: Comparison of TF×IDF, TextRank and Logistic regression for different ranking strategies when extracting a maximum of 5 and 10 keyphrases. Results are expressed as a percentage of precision (P), recall (R) and f-measure (F). † indicates significance at the 0.05 level using Student's t-test.

Normalizing the candidate scores by their lengths (`norm`) produces shorter candidates but does not limit the number of over-generation errors. As we can see from the example in Table 2, 9 out of 10 extracted keyphrases are containing the word *nugget*. Our ILP model removes these redundant keyphrases by controlling the impact of each word on the set of extracted keyphrases. The resulting set of keyphrases is more diverse and thus increases the coverage of the topics addressed in the document.

Note that the reported results are not on par with keyphrase extraction systems that use ad-hoc pre-processing, involve structural features and leverage external resources. Rather our goal in this work is to demonstrate a simple and intuitive model for reducing over-generation errors.

TF×IDF + `sum` (P = 0.1)
advertis bid; certain advertis budget; keyword bid; convex hull landscap; budget optim bid; **uniform bid strategi**; advertis slot; advertis campaign; ward advertis; searchbas advertis
TF×IDF + `norm` (P = 0.2)
advertis; advertis bid; **keyword**; keyword bid; landscap; advertis slot; advertis campaign; ward advertis; searchbas advertis; advertis random
TF×IDF + `ilp` (P = 0.4)
click; **advertis**; uniform bid; landscap; **auction**; convex hull; **keyword**; **budget optim**; single-bid strategi; queri

Table 2: Example of the top-10 extracted keyphrases for the document J-3 of the SemEval dataset. Keyphrases are stemmed and whose that match reference keyphrases are marked bold.

4 Related Work

In recent years, keyphrase extraction has attracted considerable attention and many different approaches were proposed. Generally speaking, keyphrase extraction methods can be divided into two main categories: supervised and unsupervised approaches.

Supervised approaches treat keyphrase extraction as a binary classification task, where each phrase is labeled as keyphrase or non-keyphrase (Witten et al., 1999; Turney, 2000; Kim and Kan, 2009; Lopez and Romary, 2010). Unsupervised approaches usually rank phrases by importance and select the top-ranked ones as keyphrases. Methods for ranking phrases include graph-based ranking (Mihalcea and Tarau, 2004; Wan and Xiao, 2008a; Wan and Xiao, 2008b; Bougouin et al., 2013; Boudin, 2013), topic-based clustering (Liu et al., 2009; Liu et al., 2010; Bougouin et al., 2013), statistical models (Paukkeri and Honkela, 2010; El-Beltagy and Rafea, 2010) and language modeling (Tomokiyo and Hurst, 2003).

The work of (Ding et al., 2011) is perhaps the closest to our present work. They proposed an ILP formulation of the keyphrase extraction problem that combines TF×IDF and position features in an objective function subject to constraints of coherence and coverage. In their model, coherence is measured by Mutual Information and coverage is estimated using Latent Dirichlet Allocation (LDA) (Blei et al., 2003). Their work differs from ours in that (1) it is phrased-based and thus does not penalize redundant keyphrases, and (2) it requires estimating a large number of hyperparameters which makes it difficult to generalize.

5 Conclusion and Future Work

In this paper, we proposed an ILP formulation for keyphrase extraction that reduces over-generation errors by weighting keyphrase candidates as a set rather than independently. In our model, keyphrases are selected according to their component words, and the weight of each unique word is counted only once. Experiments show a substantial improvement over commonly used word-based ranking approaches using either supervised and unsupervised weighting schemes.

In future work, we intend to extend our model to include word relatedness through the use of association measures. By doing so, we expect to better differentiate semantically related keyphrase candidates according to the association strength between their component words.

Acknowledgments

This work was partially supported by the GOLEM project (grant of CNRS PEPS FaSciDo 2015, `http://boudinfl.github.io/GOLEM/`). We thank the anonymous reviewers, Adrien Bougouin and Evgeny Gurevsky for their insightful comments.

References

Gábor Berend. 2011. Opinion expression mining by exploiting keyphrase extraction. In *Proceedings of 5th International Joint Conference on Natural Language Processing*, pages 1162–1170, Chiang Mai, Thailand, November. Asian Federation of Natural Language Processing.

David M. Blei, Andrew Y. Ng, and Michael I. Jordan. 2003. Latent dirichlet allocation. *J. Mach. Learn. Res.*, 3:993–1022, March.

Florian Boudin. 2013. A comparison of centrality measures for graph-based keyphrase extraction. In *Proceedings of the Sixth International Joint Conference on Natural Language Processing*, pages 834–838, Nagoya, Japan, October. Asian Federation of Natural Language Processing.

Adrien Bougouin, Florian Boudin, and Béatrice Daille. 2013. Topicrank: Graph-based topic ranking for keyphrase extraction. In *Proceedings of the Sixth International Joint Conference on Natural Language Processing*, pages 543–551, Nagoya, Japan, October. Asian Federation of Natural Language Processing.

Zhuoye Ding, Qi Zhang, and Xuanjing Huang. 2011. Keyphrase extraction from online news using binary integer programming. In *Proceedings of 5th International Joint Conference on Natural Language Processing*, pages 165–173, Chiang Mai, Thailand, November. Asian Federation of Natural Language Processing.

Samhaa R. El-Beltagy and Ahmed Rafea. 2010. Kp-miner: Participation in semeval-2. In *Proceedings of the 5th International Workshop on Semantic Evaluation*, pages 190–193, Uppsala, Sweden, July. Association for Computational Linguistics.

Dan Gillick and Benoit Favre. 2009. A scalable global model for summarization. In *Proceedings of the Workshop on Integer Linear Programming for Natural Language Processing*, pages 10–18, Boulder, Colorado, June. Association for Computational Linguistics.

Kazi Saidul Hasan and Vincent Ng. 2010. Conundrums in unsupervised keyphrase extraction: Making sense of the state-of-the-art. In *Coling 2010: Posters*, pages 365–373, Beijing, China, August. Coling 2010 Organizing Committee.

Kazi Saidul Hasan and Vincent Ng. 2014. Automatic keyphrase extraction: A survey of the state of the art. In *Proceedings of the 52nd Annual Meeting of the Association for Computational Linguistics (Volume 1: Long Papers)*, pages 1262–1273, Baltimore, Maryland, June. Association for Computational Linguistics.

Kai Hong and Ani Nenkova. 2014. Improving the estimation of word importance for news multi-document summarization. In *Proceedings of the 14th Conference of the European Chapter of the Association for Computational Linguistics*, pages 712–721, Gothenburg, Sweden, April. Association for Computational Linguistics.

Anette Hulth and Beáta B. Megyesi. 2006. A study on automatically extracted keywords in text categorization. In *Proceedings of the 21st International Conference on Computational Linguistics and 44th Annual Meeting of the Association for Computational Linguistics*, pages 537–544, Sydney, Australia, July. Association for Computational Linguistics.

Samir Khuller, Anna Moss, and Joseph (Seffi) Naor. 1999. The budgeted maximum coverage problem. *Information Processing Letters*, 70(1):39 – 45.

Su Nam Kim and Min-Yen Kan. 2009. Re-examining automatic keyphrase extraction approaches in scientific articles. In *Proceedings of the Workshop on Multiword Expressions: Identification, Interpretation, Disambiguation and Applications*, pages 9–16, Singapore, August. Association for Computational Linguistics.

Su Nam Kim, Olena Medelyan, Min-Yen Kan, and Timothy Baldwin. 2010. Semeval-2010 task 5 : Automatic keyphrase extraction from scientific articles. In *Proceedings of the 5th International Workshop on Semantic Evaluation*, pages 21–26, Uppsala, Sweden, July. Association for Computational Linguistics.

Marina Litvak and Mark Last. 2008. Graph-based keyword extraction for single-document summarization. In *Coling 2008: Proceedings of the workshop Multi-source Multilingual Information Extraction and Summarization*, pages 17–24, Manchester, UK, August. Coling 2008 Organizing Committee.

Zhiyuan Liu, Peng Li, Yabin Zheng, and Maosong Sun. 2009. Clustering to find exemplar terms for keyphrase extraction. In *Proceedings of the 2009 Conference on Empirical Methods in Natural Language Processing*, pages 257–266, Singapore, August. Association for Computational Linguistics.

Zhiyuan Liu, Wenyi Huang, Yabin Zheng, and Maosong Sun. 2010. Automatic keyphrase extraction via topic decomposition. In *Proceedings of the 2010 Conference on Empirical Methods in Natural Language Processing*, pages 366–376, Cambridge, MA, October. Association for Computational Linguistics.

Zhiyuan Liu, Xinxiong Chen, Yabin Zheng, and Maosong Sun. 2011. Automatic keyphrase extraction by bridging vocabulary gap. In *Proceedings of the Fifteenth Conference on Computational Natural Language Learning*, pages 135–144, Portland, Oregon, USA, June. Association for Computational Linguistics.

Patrice Lopez and Laurent Romary. 2010. Humb: Automatic key term extraction from scientific articles in grobid. In *Proceedings of the 5th International Workshop on Semantic Evaluation*, pages 248–251, Uppsala, Sweden, July. Association for Computational Linguistics.

Rada Mihalcea and Paul Tarau. 2004. Textrank: Bringing order into texts. In Dekang Lin and Dekai Wu, editors, *Proceedings of EMNLP 2004*, pages 404–411, Barcelona, Spain, July. Association for Computational Linguistics.

Thuy Dung Nguyen and Minh-Thang Luong. 2010. Wingnus: Keyphrase extraction utilizing document logical structure. In *Proceedings of the 5th International Workshop on Semantic Evaluation*, pages 166–169, Uppsala, Sweden, July. Association for Computational Linguistics.

Mari-Sanna Paukkeri and Timo Honkela. 2010. Likey: Unsupervised language-independent keyphrase extraction. In *Proceedings of the 5th International Workshop on Semantic Evaluation*, pages 162–165, Uppsala, Sweden, July. Association for Computational Linguistics.

Martin F Porter. 1980. An algorithm for suffix stripping. *Program*, 14(3):130–137.

Karen Spärck Jones. 1972. A statistical interpretation of term specificity and its application in retrieval. *Journal of Documentation*, 28:11–21.

Takashi Tomokiyo and Matthew Hurst. 2003. A language model approach to keyphrase extraction. In *Proceedings of the ACL 2003 Workshop on Multiword Expressions: Analysis, Acquisition and Treatment - Volume 18*, MWE '03, pages 33–40, Stroudsburg, PA, USA. Association for Computational Linguistics.

Kristina Toutanova, Dan Klein, Christopher D. Manning, and Yoram Singer. 2003. Feature-Rich Part-of-Speech Tagging with a Cyclic Dependency Network. In *Proceedings of the 2003 Conference of the North American Chapter of the Association for Computational Linguistics: Human Language Technology - Volume 1 (NAACL)*, pages 173–180, Stroudsburg, PA, USA. Association for Computational Linguistics.

Peter D Turney. 2000. Learning algorithms for keyphrase extraction. *Information Retrieval*, 2(4):303–336.

Xiaojun Wan and Jianguo Xiao. 2008a. Collabrank: Towards a collaborative approach to single-document keyphrase extraction. In *Proceedings of the 22nd International Conference on Computational Linguistics (Coling 2008)*, pages 969–976, Manchester, UK, August. Coling 2008 Organizing Committee.

Xiaojun Wan and Jianguo Xiao. 2008b. Single document keyphrase extraction using neighborhood knowledge. In *Proceedings of the 23rd National Conference on Artificial Intelligence - Volume 2*, AAAI'08, pages 855–860. AAAI Press.

Ian H. Witten, Gordon W. Paynter, Eibe Frank, Carl Gutwin, and Craig G. Nevill-Manning. 1999. Kea: Practical automatic keyphrase extraction. In *Proceedings of the Fourth ACM Conference on Digital Libraries*, DL '99, pages 254–255, New York, NY, USA. ACM.

TwittDict: Extracting Social Oriented Keyphrase Semantics from Twitter

Suppawong Tuarob[†], **Wanghuan Chu**[‡], **Dong Chen**[§], **and Conrad S Tucker**[♯]
[†]Faculty of Information and Communication Technology, Mahidol University, Thailand
[‡] Department of Statistics, [§]Information Sciences and Technology,
[♯]Industrial and Manufacturing Engineering, Pennsylvania State University, USA
`suppawong.tuarob@gmail.com`, `{wxc228,duc196,ctucker4}@psu.edu`

Abstract

Social media not only carries information that is up-to-date, but also bears the wisdom of the crowd. In social media, new words are developed everyday, including slangs, combinations of existing terms, entity names, etc. These terms are initially used in small communities, which can later grow popular and become new standards. The ability to early recognize the existence and understand the meanings of these terms can prove to be crucial, especially to emergence detection applications. We present an ongoing research work that investigates the use of topical analysis to extract semantic of terms in social media. In particular, the proposed method extracts semantically related words associated with a target word from a corpus of tweets. We provide preliminary, anecdotal results comprising the semantic extraction of five different keywords.

1 Introduction

Multiple applications built upon social media data have emerged and recently gained attention from a wide range of research fields. For example, public surveillance systems have shown success in employing Twitter data to detect the emergence of diseases (Tuarob et al., 2013b; Tuarob et al., 2014), emergency needs during natural disasters (Caragea et al., 2011), and even changes in product trends (Tuarob and Tucker, 2015c; Tuarob and Tucker, 2015a). Regardless of such appealing applications, tremendous challenges exist in employing traditional natural language processing techniques to handle social media data. Most of the issues with social media involve language creativity and noise, such as non-standard terms or symbolic expressions, caused by the users. Languages in social media evolve rapidly as the users have the freedom to express their opinions in colloquial, everyday languages. Some social media services such as Twitter limit the length of each message, that even challenge the users to express their complete thoughts in a compressed manner, resulting in creativity that would be considered noise by most traditional NLP techniques. This language evolution can be classified into two categories: grammatical alteration and word distortion. Grammatical alteration involves incomplete sentences (e.g. `'Dance Practice All Day Hit Up The iPhone4 (:'`), omitting words or part of words (e.g. `'[Does] Anyone have suggestions for [an] iPhone 4 mic?'`), and developing new terms (e.g. `'I totally fricken agree!'`). Word distortion involves modifying existing terms to deviate from the original meanings or to encode a phrase into a single word, such as `looooooove` (much love) and `lol` (laugh out loud). Besides the language evolution, noise is also considered a norm in social media. The sources of such noise include the use of symbolic representations (e.g. `':)'`) and typographical errors (both by intention and unintention). Both language evolution and noises produce non-standard terms, words not defined in a standard dictionary. Moreover, non-standard terms may refer to proper nouns, or entity names, e.g. *Xbox*, *Microsoft*, and *Peking*. These non-standard terms pose challenges to existing semantic interpretation techniques, especially those dependent on dictionary look-up of terms.

Text normalization techniques such as those utilizing noisy channel models (Cook and Stevenson, 2009; Xue et al., 2011) rely on the assumption that a non-standard term has its equivalent standard form (e.g. *love* ⇒ *looooove*). With such an assumption, the algorithms aim to reverse the transformation process and seek the original

Proceedings of the ACL 2015 Workshop on Novel Computational Approaches to Keyphrase Extraction, pages 25–31,
Beijing, China, July 30, 2015. ©2015 Association for Computational Linguistics

form of a non-standard term. These algorithms, however, would fail if a term is newly developed and does not have a counterpart standard form (for example, `'swine flu'`, `'linsanity'`, `'Tweeps'`, etc.).

In particular, we present *TwittDict*, a model for semantic exploration of unknown terms in social media. Specifically, the method first identifies different topics discussed in the social media corpus. It assumes that a given term is associated with one or more topics, which then allows the mapping between such a term with relevant topically represented terms. Though multiple works have shown success on semantic annotation of unknown terms, these works target the domain of traditional documents where noise and language evolution are not taken into account. A preliminary case study that uses Twitter data to extract semantically relevant terms from a set of chosen five target terms is presented.

2 Background and Related Work

Use of social media, such as collaboratively edited knowledge databases (Wikipedia[1]), blogs and microblogs (Biyani et al., 2014), content communities (YouTube[2]), and social networking sites (Facebook[3]) (Kaplan and Haenlein, 2009), has grown at a prodigious rate. According to Nielsen's report[4], the total amount of time spent by the U.S. population on social media in 2012 was 520.1 billion minutes, a 21% increase from the previous year. This results in the creation and diffusion of a huge amount of information on social media everyday, including news, knowledge, opinions, and emotions. Different groups use social media for different reasons. For instance, companies can use social media to gather customer feedback and conduct market research and reputation management. Governmental organizations can spread news and gather public opinions. Meanwhile, the wealth of information on social media contributes to the collective wisdom and can be used to predict real-world outcomes such as stock prices (Bollen et al., 2011), flu trends (Lampos et al., 2010), and product sales (Tuarob and Tucker, 2013). To realize the potential of social media, the first step is to select relevant information, which requires an understanding of language evolution on social media. One aspect of such evolution is the creation and use of new terms aiming at describing timely events or new social phenomenon. Many of these terms are too new to be indexed by standard dictionaries or Wikipedia, and the results returned by popular search engines like Google[5] can be obscure and unstructured. Therefore, we seek to use social community knowledge to extract term semantics which provide better understanding on the language evolution.

[1] http://www.wikipedia.org/
[2] https://www.youtube.com/
[3] https://www.facebook.com/
[4] http://www.nielsensocial.com/

2.0.1 Semantic Discovery of Terms

Weischedel et al. (1993) had success in employing probabilistic models to discover unknown terms and annotate them with parts of speech. Daniel et al. (1999) proposed a named entity recognition (NER) algorithm which categorizes a proper noun into one of the 3 predefined categories: Location, Person, and Organization. Besides Daniel et al's work, other NER algorithms such as (Chieu and Ng, 2002) achieved similar goals. These solutions rely on the assumption that a proper noun must fall into one of the predefined categories, while it is ubiquitous to see new categories of terms emerge from social media. Moreover, these algorithms require the data to adhere to standard English grammar. This requirement is hardly satisfied in social media. Fellbaum described *Wordnet*[6] a lexical database for English vocabulary that provides a set of synonyms (synset) for a given word. However, such database is constructed manually and only contains standard dictionary words, while our solution is fully automatic and can be applied to standard and non-standard terms that appear in social media.

2.0.2 Quantifying Unknown Terms in Social Media Data

Dealing with non-standard terms can be cumbersome. Dictionary-based approaches tend to fail when facing such unknown terms since they basically do not exist and cannot be looked up. Cook and Stevenson (2009) identified 10 different ways in which a term can be distorted in mobile text messaging. They proposed a noisy channel unsupervised model to translate a non-standard term into its standard version. Xue et al. (2011) proposed a similar channel-based model to translate a non-standard term into its standard form in the

[5] https://www.google.com/
[6] http://wordnet.princeton.edu/

Twitter domain. These algorithms assume that an unknown term can be mapped one-to-one to its standard form. Unfortunately, the presence of newly generated terms naturally found in social media violate such an assumption, simply because these terms are newly developed and hence do not have their standard forms. These newly developed terms include social slangs, trending words, and names of entities.

Lund and Burgess (1996) attempted to explore the semantic of terms by generating the term occurrence network. A term is annotated with its highly related terms based on the distances in the network. Though their algorithm treats a document as a bag of words (hence does not rely on sentence structures), the algorithm produces meaningful results when the data is high-dimensional and dense. Such properties result in a strong and meaningful co-occurrence relationship. However, each message in social media is usually represented with a short text, resulting in high-dimensional but sparse data. Consequently, such data sparsity would impede the co-occurrence relationship.

3 Methodology

Topic models (Blei and Lafferty, 2009) are powerful tools to study latent patterns in text. The semantic of an unknown word is highly related to the topics associated with the text that contains it. Moreover, identified topics can be considered as representatives of the semantic. While one document might only have a limited number of topics associated with it, the collection of a large amount of documents containing the unknown term can provide more thorough and comprehensive understanding. Therefore, topic models can be applied to extract the semantics of unknown terms with large enough collection of documents. Social media such as Twitter usually adopts the use of newly developed terms at a very fast rate. Social media users tweet about topics related to the unknown terms based on their subjective understanding. Different tweets may present different meanings towards a single term. While a single tweet lacks the information to provide the full semantics of the term, a collection of all the tweets containing the term would give a much larger and clearer picture of the semantics. Therefore, topic models can be applied on social media to extract word semantics in terms of collective wisdom and social knowledge.

In this study, we choose the Latent Dirichlet Allocation (LDA) (Blei et al., 2003) to model topical variation due to its flexibility and richness in the results. We use Twitter data as a case study, hence the name *TwittDict* is devised. Note that our algorithm can also be applied to other social media such as Facebook and Google+, as long as the medium of communication is in textual forms and community structures exist. In this section, we first briefly review our problem and introduce the LDA model, and then discuss how we filter the related tweets and how we apply the LDA to extract word semantics.

3.1 Problem Definition

Given a query word, TwittDict outputs a list of related words associated with it. The output words are ranked according to their relevance to the input term. Specifically, let $D_t = \{d_1, d_2, ..., d_n\}$ be the set of tweets, where each tweet $d_i \in D_t$ is a bag of words, W the vocabulary extracted from D_t, and w_t the query word. The proposed algorithm aims to output a ranked list of K words which are semantically relevant to w_t. For example, given a word `'Linsanity'`, the proposed algorithm would return a ranked list of semantically relevant words {`basketball, player, insanity, scholarship`} (with $K = 4$) as the output.

3.2 Latent Dirichlet Allocation

In text mining, the Latent Dirichlet Allocation (LDA) is a generative model that allows a document to be represented by a mixture of topics. The basic intuition of LDA for topic modeling is that an author has a set of topics in mind when writing a document. A topic is defined as a distribution of terms. The author then chooses a set of terms from the topics to compose the document. With such assumption, the whole document can be represented using a mixture of different topics. LDA serves as a means to trace back the topics in the author's mind before the document is written. Mathematically, the LDA model is described as follows:

$$P(w_i|d) = \sum_{j=1}^{|Z|} P(w_i|z_i = j) \cdot P(z_i = j|d). \quad (1)$$

$P(w_i|d)$ is the probability of term w_i being in document d. z_i is the latent (hidden) topic. $|Z|$ is the number of all topics, which needs to be predetermined. $P(w_i|z_i = j)$ is the probability of term w_i being in topic j. $P(z_i = j|d)$ is the probability of picking a term from topic j in the document d.

Essentially, the aim of LDA model is to find $P(z|d)$, the topic distribution of document d, with each topic described by the distribution over all terms $P(w|z)$.

After the topics are modeled, we can assign a distribution of topics to a given document using a technique called *inference*. A document then can be represented by a vector of numbers, each of which represents the probability of the document belonging to a topic:

$$\text{Infer}(d, Z) = \langle z_1, z_2, ..., z_Q \rangle; |Z| = Q,$$

where Z is a set of topics, d is a document, and z_i is a probability of the document d falling into topic i. We use the Latent Dirichlet Allocation algorithm to generate topics in our model since it allows a topic to be represented by a distribution of terms, enabling the method to propagate the relevance from the target term to the underlying terms that compose the relevant topics.

3.3 Data Preprocessing

Twitter data is collected using the Twitter API. The textual information in each tweet is first lowercased, then usernames, stopwords, punctuations, numbers, and URLs are removed. While using the wealth of information on Twitter to understand an unknown term, the first step is to filter in tweets that are related to such a term. The most intuitive collection consists of all the tweets that contain the target word and treats each single tweet as a document, which we call the basis setting. However, there are some special characteristics of Twitter messages that we want to consider for modifications and improvements. First, there is limited information within each tweet because of the 140-character restriction, and the average length of tweets is even smaller. This is quite different from the traditional uses of the LDA where input documents are rich (e.g., research articles, newspaper, etc), and hence generated topics are quite intuitive and meaningful. Second, other information in tweets such as *retweet* (`RT`), *reply* (`@username`) and *hashtag* (`#`) exist, which can be used more appropriately instead of just being deleted or treated as a plain word. To overcome the drawbacks and make better use of Twitter features, we consider improving the basis setting by expanding the collection of tweets using *reply* and *hashtag*. *Reply* refers to those tweets that start with `@username` and comment on other tweets. For the tweet that contains the unknown term, its *reply* tweets make comments on the same or other related topics. Although these tweets might not contain the target word, it is reasonable to assume that they should be in similar semantic as the original tweet thus providing additional information. Therefore, we will expand the collection of tweets by combining all the *reply* tweets to the original one which contains the target term. *Hashtag* can also be used to find related tweets. People use the hashtag symbol # before a relevant keyword or phrase without space in the tweets to facilitate automatic categorization and search. These hashtags can be viewed as topical markers, serving as indications to the context or the core idea of the tweet. Tweets with the same hashtag share similar topics. Therefore, we use hashtags in the basis tweet to find all the other tweets that have at least one of these hashtags, which also enriches the information in the collection.

3.4 Retrieving Related Words

Mathematically, given a target document corpus $D_t = \langle d_1, d_2, ..., d_n \rangle$ (as described in Section 3.3), vocabulary $W = \langle w_1, w_2, ..., w_m \rangle$, and target word w_t, our algorithm outputs a ranked list $W_K^* = \langle w_1, w_2, ..., w_K \rangle$, where $w_i \in W$, of K words relevant to w_t.

Our algorithm comprises two main steps:

1. $P(w|w_t, W, D_t)$, the likelihood probability of the word w being relevant to the target word w_t, is computed for each $w \in W$.

2. Return top K words ranked by the likelihood probability.

In general, $P(w|w_t, W, D_t)$ is computed by weighted averaging of the posterior probability of $P(w|Z)$ across the documents in D, where Z is the set of topics:

$$P(w|w_t, W, D_t) = \sum_{z \in Z} P(z|D_t) \cdot P(w|z), \quad (2)$$

where $P(w|z)$ is the posterior probability of the word w being in topic z, computed in Equation 1. $P(z|D_t)$ serves as the weight of the topic z, computed by averaging out the topic probability $P(z|d)$ across all documents in D_t:

$$P(z|D_t) = \frac{1}{|D_t|} \sum_{d \in D_t} P(z|d), \quad (3)$$

where $P(z|d)$ is computed based on Equation 1. Hence:

$$P(w|w_t, W, D_t) = \frac{1}{|D_t|} \sum_{z \in Z} \sum_{d \in D_t} P(z|d) \cdot P(w|z) \quad (4)$$

4 Evaluation

TwittDict is evaluated against the baseline which utilizes a variant of word co-occurrence to retrieve relevant keywords. Church et al. had success on using the mutual information to extract semantic related terms (1990). Furthermore, Tuarob and Tucker had used the word co-occurrence network to explicate implicit semantics in product related tweets (2015b). Here, the word co-occurrence network is constructed from the tweet corpus. The co-occurrence network is an undirected graph where each node is a distinct word, and each edge weight represents the frequency of co-occurrence. The edge weights can be used directly to compute $P(x, y)$, where x and y are co-occurred words. Given a target word w_t, a corpus of tweets T, and vocabulary $W = \langle w_1, w_2, ..., w_m \rangle$, the baseline algorithm outputs a ranked list $W_K^B = \langle w_1, w_2, ..., w_K \rangle$, where $w_i \in W$, of K words relevant to w_t. The algorithm assigns a co-occurrence based score to each word, and rank them by such a score. In this work, we experiment with three variations of co-occurrence based scores: Mutual Information (MI), Co-Frequency (CoF), and Co-Frequency Inverse Document Frequency (CoF-IDF):

$$Score_{MI}(w_t, w) = \log_2 \frac{P(w_t, w)}{P(w_t) \cdot P(w)} \quad (5)$$

$$Score_{CoF}(w_t, w) = P(w_t, w) \quad (6)$$

$$Score_{CoF-IDF}(w_t, w) = P(w_t, w) \cdot IDF(w, T) \quad (7)$$

5 Preliminary Case Study

We experiment our methodology with Twitter data and a set of manually selected words. Twitter data is used due to its ubiquitousness and public availability. Note that, our methodology can expand to other types of social media such as Facebook and Google+ if the data is available.

5.1 Twitter Data

Twitter is a microblog service that allows its users to send and read text messages of up to 140 characters, known as tweets. The Twitter dataset used in this research study comprises roughly 700 million tweets in the United States during the period of 19 months, from March 2011 to September 2012.

5.2 Anecdotal Results

A set of five target words ($Obama$, $Pandora$, $Xbox$, $Glee$, and $Zombie$) are used to test our proposed algorithm against one of the baseline with Co-frequency scores. TwittDict employs the LDA implementation in Mallet[7], with 100 topics and runs for 1,000 iterations using Gibb's Sampling. Due to the limitation on the computational time, TwittDict currently only models topics from a tweet corpus collected in March 2011. For the baseline, we first index the whole tweet corpus using Apache Lucene[8], then use the same library to compute word frequency. Table 1 lists the results.

From the preliminary results, TwittDict is able to extract highly meaningful words related to the target words, while the baseline contain a mixture of both related and generally spurious words. Note that, TwittDict only uses one month's worth (5.26%) of the available Twitter data, as opposed to the baseline which uses the whole collection of tweets. It is our belief that, with more Twitter data, TwittDict could even provide a wider variety and higher in semantics of lexicons.

6 Conclusions and Future Works

By leveraging natural language processing techniques and specific features in social media, we have described our ongoing development of *TwittDict*, a system to identify the social-oriented semantic meaning of unknown words. Such a system could prove to be useful as a building block for emergence detection systems where early recognition of new terms/concepts is crucial. We illustrated through anecdotal results using Twitter data to identify semantic meanings of five terms, that our method is not only achieving promising results, but also urging us to explore further into improving our methods along with conducting rigorous user and automatic evaluations such as (Tuarob et al., 2013a; Tuarob et al.,

[7]http://mallet.cs.umass.edu/
[8]http://lucene.apache.org/

Table 1: Preliminary results of 5 test words using both the baseline (CoF scores) and TwittDict.

Word	Obama		Pandora		Xbox		Glee		Zombie	
/Rank	Co-Freq	TwittDict	Co-Freq	TwittDict	Co-Freq	TwittDict	Co-Freq	TwittDict	Co-Freq	TwittDict
1	president	president	flow	station	live	live	watching	watching	apocalypse	apocalypse
2	vote	libya	station	radio	play	play	love	tonight	feel	lol
3	michelle	people	listening	listening	playing	kinect	watch	episode	lol	www
4	romney	war	radio	lol	got	lol	tonight	watch	day	movie
5	barack	bush	love	music	lol	playing	episode	love	dead	today
6	lol	barack	point	playing	time	game	season	song	mode	feel
7	don	don	tonight	song	need	games	project	time	sleep	movies
8	america	news	commercials	love	game	time	lol	good	walking	love
9	love	pres	playing	time	add	black	time	show	time	time
10	speech	time	lol	songs	don	back	omg	lol	today	back
11	fuck	gop	song	good	kinect	don	cast	songs	movie	zombies
12	got	white	time	shit	buy	buy	wait	don	night	band
13	dnc	america	listen	listen	games	good	song	night	zombies	dead
14	voting	oil	songs	day	fuck	day	good	cast	don	day
15	people	world	shit	today	shit	ops	don	amazing	love	mode
16	good	tcot	night	play	wanna	gamertag	amazing	omg	good	horror
17	campaign	japan	music	work	day	follow	night	week	shit	good
18	years	administration	jamming	flow	love	win	version	version	rob	house
19	win	house	got	tonight	controller	controller	excited	awesome	walkingdead	plays
20	osama	gas	sleep	night	haha	love	week	music	need	atomic

2015). There is plenty of room to improve *TwittDict*. In the current case study, we only used Twitter data during Mar 2011. This specific period of time may bring about bias towards the result. To avoid such bias, we need to test data in different times and geographical regions. This will shed light on how meanings of a term evolve temporally and spatially. When we were conducting the small case study, we noticed that the results were highly dependent on the time period, as Twitter users usually tweet about the current social phenomena. This change reflects the evolvement of social events and community knowledge. We are considering giving users the freedom to specify the time period during which a term is defined. Furthermore, we would explore methods for user evaluations. We would recruit human participants to give feedback about their experience. Real user experience is of great value for us to see whether and how community knowledge from social media truly helps them to better understand the unknown, emerging concepts. Finally, we would like to compare our method against well-established baseline such as (Turney et al., 2010) and (Mikolov et al., 2013).

References

Daniel M. Bikel, Richard Schwartz, and Ralph M. Weischedel. 1999. An algorithm that learns what's in a name. *Mach. Learn.*, 34(1-3):211–231, February.

Prakhar Biyani, Cornelia Caragea, Prasenjit Mitra, and John Yen. 2014. Identifying emotional and informational support in online health communities.

David M Blei and J Lafferty. 2009. Topic models. *Text mining: classification, clustering, and applications*, 10:71.

David M. Blei, Andrew Y. Ng, and Michael I. Jordan. 2003. Latent dirichlet allocation. *J. Mach. Learn. Res.*, 3:993–1022, March.

Johan Bollen, Huina Mao, and Xiaojun Zeng. 2011. Twitter mood predicts the stock market. *Journal of Computational Science*, 2(1):1–8.

C. Caragea, N. McNeese, A. Jaiswal, G. Traylor, H.W. Kim, P. Mitra, D. Wu, A.H. Tapia, L. Giles, B.J. Jansen, et al. 2011. Classifying text messages for the haiti earthquake. In *ISCRAM '11*.

Hai Leong Chieu and Hwee Tou Ng. 2002. Named entity recognition: a maximum entropy approach using global information. COLING '02, pages 1–7, Stroudsburg, PA, USA. Association for Computational Linguistics.

Kenneth Ward Church and Patrick Hanks. 1990. Word association norms, mutual information, and lexicography. *Comput. Linguist.*, 16(1):22–29, March.

Paul Cook and Suzanne Stevenson. 2009. An unsupervised model for text message normalization. CALC '09, pages 71–78, Stroudsburg, PA, USA. Association for Computational Linguistics.

Andreas M. Kaplan and Michael Haenlein. 2009. The fairyland of second life: Virtual social worlds and how to use them. *Business Horizons*, 52(6):563 – 572.

Vasileios Lampos, Tijl De Bie, and Nello Cristianini. 2010. Flu detector-tracking epidemics on twitter. In *Machine Learning and Knowledge Discovery in Databases*, pages 599–602. Springer.

Kevin Lund and Curt Burgess. 1996. Producing high-dimensional semantic spaces from lexical co-occurrence. *Behavior Research Methods*, 28(2):203–208.

Tomas Mikolov, Kai Chen, Greg Corrado, and Jeffrey Dean. 2013. Efficient estimation of word representations in vector space. *arXiv preprint arXiv:1301.3781*.

Suppawong Tuarob and Conrad S Tucker. 2013. Fad or here to stay: Predicting product market adoption and longevity using large scale, social media data. In *ASME IDETC/CIE '13*.

Suppawong Tuarob and Conrad S Tucker. 2015a. Automated discovery of lead users and latent product features by mining large scale social media networks. *Journal of Mechanical Design*.

Suppawong Tuarob and Conrad S Tucker. 2015b. A product feature inference model for mining implicit customer preferences within large scale social media networks. In *ASME IDETC/CIE '15*.

Suppawong Tuarob and Conrad S Tucker. 2015c. Quantifying product favorability and extracting notable product features using large scale social media data. *Journal of Computing and Information Science in Engineering*.

Suppawong Tuarob, Line C Pouchard, and C Lee Giles. 2013a. Automatic tag recommendation for metadata annotation using probabilistic topic modeling. JCDL '13, pages 239–248.

Suppawong Tuarob, Conrad S Tucker, Marcel Salathe, and Nilam Ram. 2013b. Discovering health-related knowledge in social media using ensembles of heterogeneous features. In *CIKM '13*, pages 1685–1690. ACM.

Suppawong Tuarob, Conrad S Tucker, Marcel Salathe, and Nilam Ram. 2014. An ensemble heterogeneous classification methodology for discovering health-related knowledge in social media messages. *Journal of biomedical informatics*, 49:255–268.

Suppawong Tuarob, Line C Pouchard, Prasenjit Mitra, and C Lee Giles. 2015. A generalized topic modeling approach for automatic document annotation. *International Journal on Digital Libraries*, 16(2):111–128.

Peter D Turney, Patrick Pantel, et al. 2010. From frequency to meaning: Vector space models of semantics. *Journal of artificial intelligence research*, 37(1):141–188.

Ralph Weischedel, Richard Schwartz, Jeff Palmucci, Marie Meteer, and Lance Ramshaw. 1993. Coping with ambiguity and unknown words through probabilistic models. *Comput. Linguist.*, 19(2):361–382, June.

Zhenzhen Xue, Dawei Yin, and Brian D Davison. 2011. Normalizing microtext. In *Proceedings of the AAAI Workshop on Analyzing Microtext*, pages 74–79.

Identification and Classification of Emotional Key Phrases from Psychological Texts

Apurba Paul
JIS College of Engineering
Kalyani,Nadia
West Bengal, India
apurba.saitech@gmail.com

Dipankar Das
Jadavpur University
188, Raja S.C. Mullick Road, Kolkata
West Bengal, India
ddas@cse.jdvu.ac.in

Abstract

Emotions, a complex state of feeling results in physical and psychological changes that influence human behavior. Thus, in order to extract the emotional key phrases from psychological texts, here, we have presented a phrase level emotion identification and classification system. The system takes pre-defined emotional statements of seven basic emotion classes (*anger, disgust, fear, guilt, joy, sadness* and *shame*) as input and extracts seven types of emotional trigrams. The trigrams were represented as Context Vectors. Between a pair of Context Vectors, an Affinity Score was calculated based on the law of gravitation with respect to different distance metrics (e.g., *Chebyshev, Euclidean* and *Hamming*). The words, Part-Of-Speech (POS) tags, TF-IDF scores, variance along with Affinity Score and ranked score of the vectors were employed as important features in a supervised classification framework after a rigorous analysis. The comparative results carried out for four different classifiers e.g., NaiveBayes, J48, Decision Tree and BayesNet show satisfactory performances.

1 Introduction

Human emotions are the most complex and unique features to be described. If we ask someone regarding emotion, he or she will reply simply that it is a '*feeling*'. Then, the obvious question that comes into our mind is about the definition of *feeling*. It is observed that such terms are difficult to define and even more difficult to understand completely. Ekman (1980) proposed six basic emotions (*anger, disgust, fear, guilt, joy* and *sadness*) that have a shared meaning on the level of facial expressions across cultures (Scherer, 1997; Scherer and Wallbott, 1994). Psychological texts contain huge number of emotional words because psychology and emotions are inter-wined, though they are different (Brahmachari et.al, 2013). A phrase that contains more than one word can be a better way of representing emotions than a single word. Thus, the emotional phrase identification and their classification from text have great importance in Natural Language Processing (NLP).

In the present work, we have extracted seven different types of emotional statements (*anger, disgust, fear, guilt, joy, sadness* and *shame*) from the Psychological corpus. Each of the emotional statements was tokenized; the tokens were grouped in trigrams and considered as Context Vectors. These Context Vectors are POS tagged and corresponding TF and TF-IDF scores were measured for considering them as important features or not. In addition, the Affinity Scores were calculated for each pair of Context Vectors based on different distance metrics (*Chebyshev, Euclidean* and *Hamming*). Such features lead to apply different classification methods like NaiveBayes, J48, Decision Tree and BayesNet and after that the results are compared.

The route map for this paper is the Related Work (Section 2), Data Preprocessing Framework (Section 3) followed by Feature Analysis and Classification framework (Section 4) and result analysis (Section 5) along with the improvement due to ranking. Finally, we have concluded the discussion (Section 6).

2 Related Work

Strapparava and Valitutti (2004) developed the WORDNET-AFFECT, a lexical resource that assigns one or more affective labels such as emotion, mood, trait, cognitive state, physical state, behavior, attitude and sensation etc to a number of

Proceedings of the ACL 2015 Workshop on Novel Computational Approaches to Keyphrase Extraction, pages 32–38,
Beijing, China, July 30, 2015. ©2015 Association for Computational Linguistics

WORDNET synsets. A detailed annotation scheme that identifies key components and properties of opinions and emotions in language has been described in (Wiebe et al., 2005). The authors in (Kobayashi et al., 2004) also developed an opinion lexicon out of their annotated corpora. Takamura et al. (2005) extracted semantic orientation of words according to the spin model, where the semantic orientation of words propagates in two possible directions like electrons. Esuli and Sebastiani's (2006) approach to develop the SentiWordNet is an adaptation to synset classification based on the training of ternary classifiers for deciding positive and negative (P-N) polarity. Each of the ternary classifiers is generated using the Semi-supervised rules.

On the other hand, Mohammad, et al., (2010) has performed an extensive analysis of the annotations to better understand the distribution of emotions evoked by terms of different parts of speech. The authors in (Das and Bandyopadhyay, 2009, 2010) created the emotion lexicon and systems for Bengali language. The development of SenticNet (Cambria et al., 2010) was inspired later by (Poria et al., 2013). The authors developed an enriched SenticNet with affective information by assigning emotion labels. Similarly, ConceptNet[1] is a multilingual knowledge base, representing words and phrases that people use and the common-sense relationships between them.

Balahur et al., (2012) had shown that the task of emotion detection from texts such as the one in the ISEAR corpus (where little or no lexical clues of affect are present) can be best tackled using approaches based on commonsense knowledge. In this sense, EmotiNet, apart from being a precise resource for classifying emotions in such examples, has the advantage of being extendable with external sources, thus increasing the recall of the methods employing it. Patra et al., (2013) adopted the Potts model for the probability modeling of the lexical network that was constructed by connecting each pair of words in which one of the two words appears in the gloss of the other.

In contrast to the previous approaches, the present task comprises of classifying the emotional phrases by forming Context Vectors and the experimentation with simple features like POS, TF-IDF and Affinity Score followed by the computation of similarities based on different distance metrics help in making decisions to correctly classify the emotional phrases.

3 Data Preprocessing Framework

3.1 Corpus Preparation

The emotional statements were collected from the ISEAR[7] (International Survey on Emotion Antecedents and Reactions) database. Each of the emotion classes contains the emotional statements given by the respondents as answers based on some predefined questions. Student respondents, both psychologists and non-psychologists were asked to report situations in which they had experienced all of the 7 major emotions (*anger, disgust, fear, guilt, joy, sadness, shame*). The final data set contains reports of 3000 respondents from 37 countries. The statements were split in sentences and tokenized into words and the statistics were presented in Table 1. It is found that only 1096 statements belong to *anger, disgust sadness* and *shame* classes whereas the *fear, guilt* and *joy* classes contain 1095, 1093 and 1094 different statements, respectively. Since each statement may contain multiple sentences, so after sentence tokenization, it is observed that the *anger* and *fear* classes contain the maximum number of sentences. Similarly, it is observed that the *anger* class contains the maximum number of tokenized words.

Emotions	Total No. of **Statements**	Total No. of **Sentences**	Total No. of **Tokenized Words**
Anger	*1096*	*1760*	*24301*
Disgust	*1096*	*1607*	*20871*
Fear	*1095*	*1760*	*22912*
Guilt	*1093*	*1718*	*22430*
Joy	*1094*	*1554*	*18851*
Sadness	*1096*	*1606*	*19480*
Shame	*1096*	*1609*	*20948*
Total	**7,666**	**11,614**	**1,49,793**

Table 1: Corpus Statistics

The tokenized words were grouped to form trigrams in order to grasp the roles of the previous and next tokens with respect to the target token. Thus, each of the trigrams was considered as a Context Window (CW) to acquire the emotional phrases. The updated version of the standard word lists of the WordNet Affect (Strapparava, and Vali-

[1] http://conceptnet5.media.mit.edu/

tutti, 2004) was collected and it is observed that the total of 2,958 affect words is present.

It is considered that, in each of the Context Windows, the first word appears as a non-affect word, second word as an affect word, and third word as a non-affect word (<NAW_1>, <AW>, <NAW_2>). It is observed from the statistics of CW as shown in Table 2 that the *anger* class contains the maximum number of trigrams (20,785) and *joy* class has the minimum number of trigrams (15,743) whereas only the *fear* class contains the maximum number of trigrams (1,573) that follow the CW pattern. A few example patterns of the CWs which follows the pattern (<NAW_1>, <AW>, <NAW_2>) are "*advices, about, problems*" (*Anger*), "*already, frightened, us" (Fear), "always, joyous, one" (Joy), "acted, cruelly, to" (Disgust)*, "*adolescent, guilt, growing*" (guilt), "*always, sad, for*" (sad) , "*and, sorry, just*" (Shame) etc.

It was observed that the stop words are mostly present in <NAW_1, AW, NAW_2> pattern where similar and dissimilar NAWs are appeared before and after their corresponding CWs. In case of *fear*, a total of 979 stop words were found in NAW_1 position and 935 stop words in NAW_2 position. It is observed that in case of *fear*, the occurrence of similar NAW before and after of CWs is only 22 in contrast to the dissimilar occurrences of 1551. Table 3 explains the statistics of similar and dissimilar NAWs along with their appearances as stop words.

3.2 Context Vector Formation

In order to identify whether the Context Windows (CWs) play any significant role in classifying emotions or not, we have mapped the Context Windows in a Vector space by representing them as vectors. We have tried to find out the semantic relation or similarity between a pair of vectors using Affinity Score which in turn takes care of different distances into consideration. Since a CW follows the pattern (NAW1, AW, NAW2), the formation of vector with respect to each of the Context Windows of each emotion class was done based on the following formula,

$$\text{Vectorization}_{(CW)} = \left[\frac{\#NAW_1}{T}, \frac{\#AW}{T}, \frac{\#NAW_2}{T}\right]$$

Where,

T= Total count of CW in an emotion class

$\#NAW_1$ = Total occurrence of a non-affect word in NAW_1 position

$\#NAW_2$ = Total occurrence of a non-affect word in NAW_2 position

#AW = Total occurrence of an affect word in AW position.

It was found that in case of *anger* emotion, a CW identified as (*always, angry, about*) corresponds to a Vector, <0.29, 10.69, 1.47>

Emotions	Total No of Trigrams	Total no of Trigrams that follows <NAW_1,AW,NAW_2> pattern (CW)
Anger	*20785*	*1356*
Disgust	*17661*	*1283*
Fear	*19392*	*1573*
Guilt	*18997*	*1298*
Joy	*15743*	*1179*
Sadness	*16270*	*1210*
Shame	*17731*	*1058*

Table 2: Trigrams and Affect Words Statistics

Emotions	Total no. of NAW_1 appeared as stop words in CW	Total no. of NAW_2 appeared as stop words in CW	Presence of similar NAW before and after of CW	Presence of dissimilar NAW before and after of CW
Anger	*825*	*871*	*26*	*1330*
Disgust	*696*	*763*	*11*	*1272*
Fear	*979*	*935*	*22*	*1551*
Guilt	*695*	*874*	*18*	*1280*
Joy	*734*	*674*	*11*	*1168*
Sadness	*733*	*753*	*22*	*1188*
Shame	*604*	*647*	*16*	*1042*

NAW_1= Non Affect $Word_1$; AW=Affect Word; NAW_2=Non Affect $Word_2$

Table 3: Statistics for similar and dissimilar NAW patterns and stop words

3.3 Affinity Score Calculation

We assume that each of the Context Vectors in an emotion class is represented in the vector space at a specific distance from the others. Thus, there must be some affinity or similarity exists between each of the Context Vectors. An Affinity Score was calculated for each pair of Context Vectors (p_u,q_v) where u = {*1,2,3,.........n*} and v = {*1,2,3,.......n*} for *n* number of vectors with respect to each of the emotion classes. The final Score is calculated using the following gravitational formula as described in (Poria et al., 2013):

$$\textbf{Score}\left(p,q\right) = \left[\frac{p * q}{\left(\textbf{dist}(p,q)\right)^{2}}\right]$$

The Score of any two context vectors p and q of an emotion class is the dot product of the vectors divided by the square of distance (*dist*) between p and q. This score was inspired by Newton's law of gravitation. This score values reflect the affinity between two context vectors p and q. Higher score implies higher affinity between p and q.

However, apart from the score values, we also calculated the median, standard deviation and inter quartile range (*iqr*) and only those context windows were considered if their *iqr* values are greater than some cutoff value selected during experiments.

3.4 Affinity Scores using Distance Metrics

In the vector space, it is needed to calculate how close the context vectors are in the space in order to conduct better classification into their respective emotion classes. The Score values were calculated for all the emotion classes with respect to different metrics of distance (*dist*) viz. *Chebyshev, Euclidean* and *Hamming*. The distance was calculated for each context vector with respect to all the vectors of the same emotion class. The distance formula is given below:

a. *Chebyshev distance* (C_d) = $max\, |x_i - y_i|$ where x_i and y_i represents two vectors.

b. *Euclidean distance* (E_d) = $\|x - y\|_2$ for vectors x and y.

c. *Hamming distance* (H_d) = $(c_{01} + c_{10}) / n$ where c_{ij} is the number of occurrence in the boolean vectors x and y and $x[k] = i$ and $y[k] = j$ for $k < n$. Hamming distance denotes the proportion of disagreeing components in x and y.

4 Feature Selection and Analysis

It is observed that the feature selection always plays an important role in building a good pattern classifier. Thus, we have employed different classifiers viz. BayesNet, J48, NaiveBayesSimple and DecisionTree associated in the WEKA tool. Based on the previous analysis, the following features were selected for developing the classification framework.

1. Affinity Scores based on C_d, E_d and H_d
2. Context Window(CW)
3. POS Tagged Context Window (PTCW)
4. POS Tagged Window (PTW)
5. TF and TF-IDF of CW
6. Variance and Standard Deviation of CW
7. Ranking Score of CW

4.1 POS Tagged Context Windows and Windows (PTCW and PTW)

The sentences were POS tagged using the Stanford POS Tagger and the POS tagged Context Windows were extracted and termed as PTCW. Similarly, the POS tag sequence from each of the PTCWs were extracted and named each as POS Tagged Window (PTW). It is observed that "*fear*" emotion class has the maximum number of CWs and unique PTCWs whereas the "*anger*" class contains the maximum number of unique PTWs. The Figure 1 as shown below represents the counts of CW, unique PTCWs and PTWs. It was noticed that the total number of CWs is 8967, total number of unique PTCW is 7609 and of unique PTW is 3117. Obviously, the number of PTCW was less than CW and number of PTW was less than PTCW, because of the uniqueness of PTCW and PTW. In Figure 2, the total counts of CW, PTCW and PTW have been shown. Some sample patterns of PTWs that occur with the maximum frequencies in three emotion classes are "VBD/RB_JJ_IN" (*anger*), "NN/VBD_VBN_NN" (*disgust*) and "VBD_VBN/JJ_IN/NN" (*fear*).

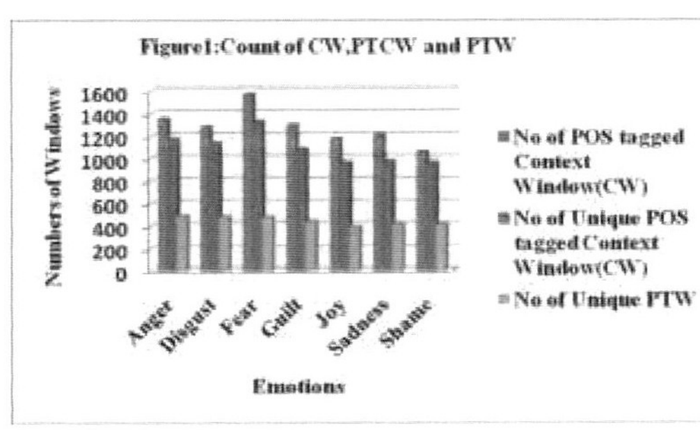

Figure 1: Count of CW, PTCW and PTW for seven emotion classes

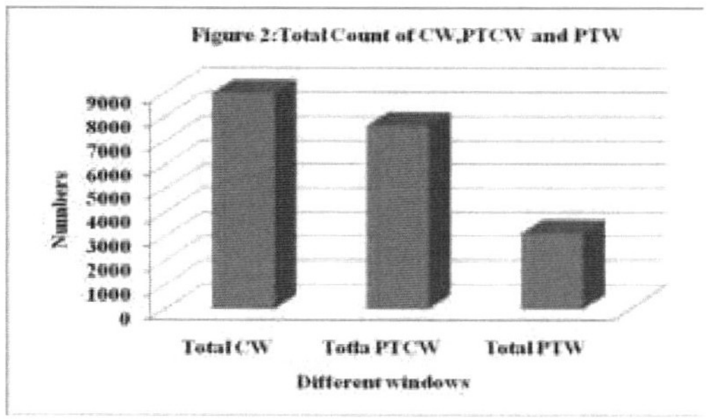

Figure 2:Total Count of CW, PTCW and PTW

4.2 TF and TF-IDF Measure

The Term Frequencies (TFs) and the Inverse Document Frequencies (IDFs) of the CWs for each of the emotion classes were calculated. In order to identify different ranges of the TF and TF-IDF scores, the minimum and maximum values of the TF and the variance of TF were calculated for each of the emotion classes. It was observed that *guilt* has the maximum scores for Max_TF and variance whereas the emotions like *anger* and *disgust* have the lowest scores for Max_TF as shown in Figure 3. Similarly, the minimum, maximum and variance of the TF-IDF values were calculated for each emotion class, separately. Again, it is found that the *guilt* emotion has the highest Max_TF-IDF and *disgust* emotion has the lowest Max_TF-IDF as shown in Figure 4.

Not only for the Context Windows (CWs), the TF and TF-IDF scores of the POS Tagged Context Windows (PTCWs) and POS Tagged Windows (PTWs) were also calculated with respect to each emotion. It was observed that, similar results were found. Variance, or second moment about the mean, is a measure of the variability (spread or dispersion) of data. A large variance indicates that the data is spread out; a small variance indicates it is clustered closely around the mean.The variance for TF_IDF of *guilt* is 0.0000456874. A few slight differences were found in the results of PTWs while calculating Max_TF , Min_TF and variance as shown in Figure 3. It was observed that *fear* emotion has the highest Max_TF and *anger* has the lowest Max_TF whereas the variance of TF for *guilt* is 0.0002435522. Similarly, Figure 4 shows that *fear* has the highest Max_TF_IDF and *anger* contains the lowest Max_TF-IDF values and the variance of TF-IDF of *fear* is 0.000922226.

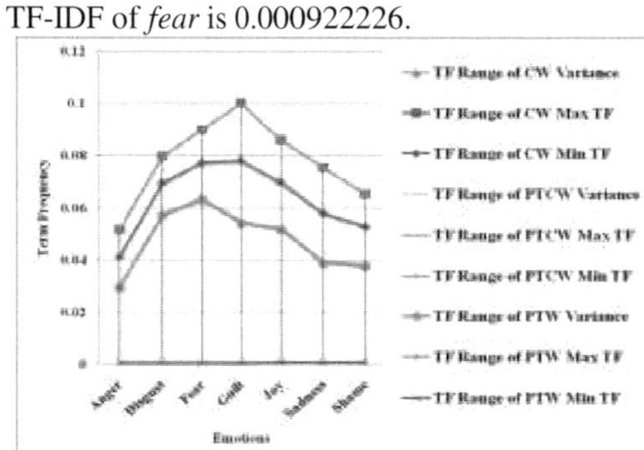

Figure 3:Variance,Max_TF,Min_TF of CW, PTCW and PTW

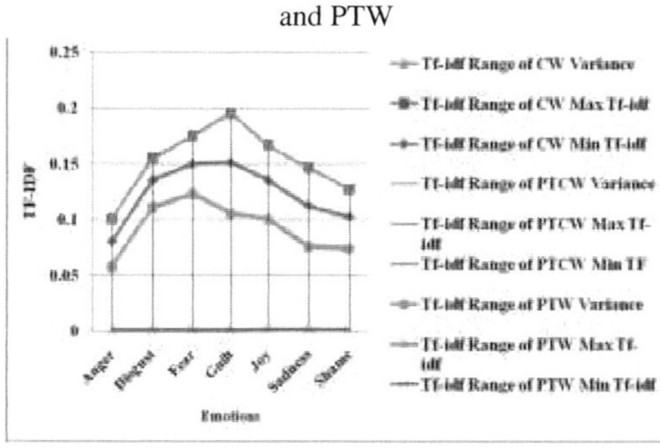

Figure 4: Variance,Max_TF-IDF, Min_TF-IDF of CW, PTCW and PTW

4.3 Ranking Score of CW

It was found that some of the Context Windows appear more than one time in the same emotion class. Thus, they were removed and a ranking score was calculated for each of the context windows. Each of the words in a context window was searched in the SentiWordnet lexicon and if found, we considered either *positive* or *negative* or both scores. The summation of the absolute scores of all the words in a Context Window is returned. The returned scores were sorted so that, in turn, each of the context windows obtains a rank in its corresponding emotion class.

All the ranks were calculated for each emotion class, successively. This rank is useful in finding the important emotional phrases from the list of CWs. Some examples from the list of top 12 important context windows according to their rank are "*much anger when*" (*anger*), "*whom love after*" (*happy*), "*felt sad about*" (*sadness*) etc.

5 Result Analysis

The accuracies of the classifiers were obtained by employing user defined test data and data for 10 fold cross validation. It is observed that when Euclidean distance was considered, the BayesNet Classifier gives 100% accuracy on the Test data and gives 97.91% of accuracy on 10-fold cross validation data. On the other hand, J48 classifier achieves 77% accuracy on Test data and 83.54% on 10-fold cross validation data whereas the NaiveBayesSimple classifier obtains 92.30% accuracy on Test data and 27.07% accuracy on 10-fold cross validation data. In the Naïve BayesSimple with 10-fold cross validation, the average Recall, Precision and F-measure values are 0.271, 0.272 and 0.264, respectively. But, the DecisionTree classifier obtains 98.30% and 98.10% accuracies on the Test data as well as 10-fold cross validation data. The comparative results are shown in Figure 5. Overall, it is observed from Figure 5 that the BayesNet classifier achieves the best results on the score data which was prepared based on the Euclidean distance. In contrast, the BayesNet achieved 99.30% accuracy on the Test data and 96.92% accuracy on 10-fold cross validation data when the Hamming distance was considered. Similarly, J48 and Naïve BayesSimple classifiers produce 93.05% and 85.41% accuracies on the Test data and 87.95% and 39.50% accuracies on 10-fold cross validation data, respectively.

From Figure 6, it is observed that the DecisionTree classifier produces the best accuracy on the score data that was found using Hamming distance. When the score values are found by using Chebyshev distance, the BayesNet classifier obtains 100% accuracy on Test data and 97.57% accuracy on 10-fold cross validation data. Similarly, J48 achieves 84.82% accuracy on the Test data and 82.75% accuracy on 10-fold cross validation data whereas NaiveBayes and DecisionTable achieve 80% , 29.85% and 98.62% ,96.93% accuracies on the Test data and 10-fold cross validatation data, respectively.

It has to be mentioned based on Figure 7 that the DecisionTree classifier performs better in comparison with all other classifiers and achieves the best result among the rest of the classifiers on affinity score data prepared based on the Chebyshev distance only.

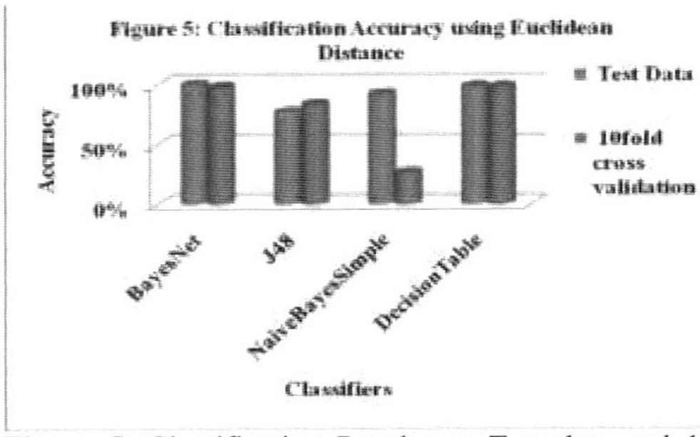

Figure 5: Classification Results on Test data and 10-fold cross validation using Euclidean distance (E_d)

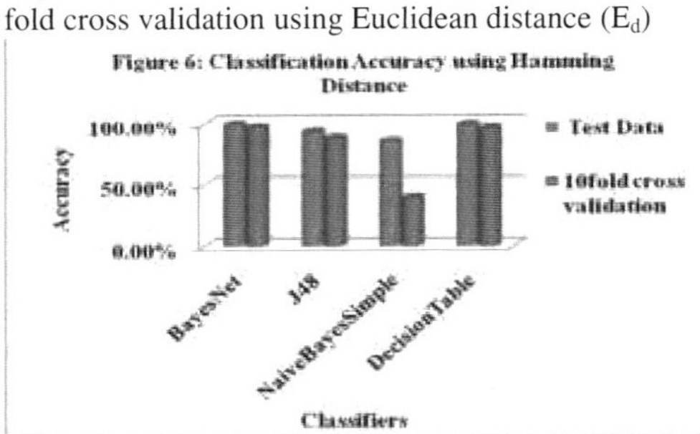

Figure 6: Classification Results on Test data and 10-fold cross validation using Hamming distance (H_d)

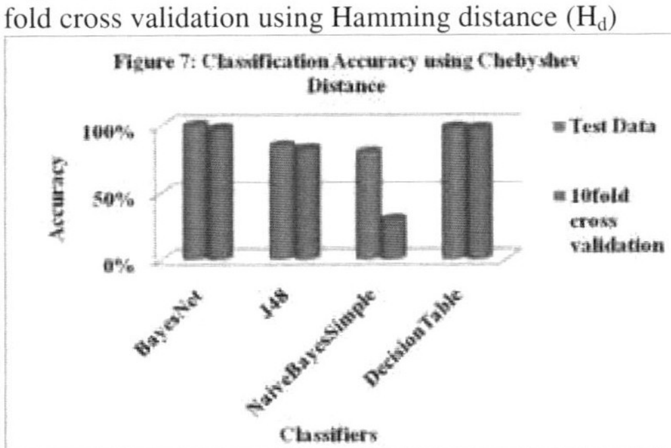

Figure 7: Classification Results on Test data and 10-fold cross validation using Chebyshev distance (C_d)

6 Conclusions and Future Works

In this paper, vector formation was done for each of the Context Windows; TF and TF-IDF measures were calculated. The calculated affinity score, depending on the distance values was inspired from Newton's law of gravitation. To classify these CWs, BayesNet, J48, NaivebayesSimple and DecisionTable classifiers.

In future, we would like to incorporate more number of lexicons to identify and classify emotional expressions. Moreover, we are planning to include associative learning process to identify some important rules for classification.

References

Balahur A , Hermida J. 2012.*Extending the EmotiNet Knowledge Base to Improve the Automatic Detection of Implicitly Expressed Emotions from Text. In Irec-conference 2012,pp-1207-1214*

Das, D. and Bandyopadhyay, S. 2009. *Word to Sentence Level Emotion Tagging for Bengali Blogs. In ACL-IJCNLP 2009 (Short Paper), pp.149-152*

Das, D. and Bandyopadhyay, S. 2010. *Developing Bengali WordNet Affect for Analyzing Emotion. ICCPOL-2010, pp. 35-40*

Ekman, P.1993. *Facial expression and emotion. American Psychologist, vol. 48(4) 384–392.*

Erik Cambria, Robert Speer, Catherine Havasi, Amir Hussain.2010. *SenticNet: A Publicly Available Semantic Resource for Opinion Mining*

Kobayashi, N., K. Inui, Y. Matsumoto, K. Tateishi, and T. Fukushima. 2004. *Collecting evaluative expressions for opinion extraction. IJCNLP.*

Mohammad S and Turney P,2010. *Emotions Evoked by Common Words and Phrases: Using Mechanical Turk to Create an Emotion Lexicon. In Proceedings of the NAACL-HLT 2010 Workshop on Computational Approaches to Analysis and Generation of Emotion in Text, June 2010, LA, California*

Patra B, Takamura H, Das D, Okumura M, and Bandyopadhyay S 2013.*Construction of Emotional Lexicon Using Potts Model. In IJCNLP 2013 pp-674-679*

Poria S, Gelbukh A, Hussain A, Howard N, Das D, Bandyopadhyay S. 2013. *Enhanced SenticNet with Affective Labels for Concept-Based Opinion Mining, IEEE Intelligent Systems, vol. 28, no. 2, pp. 31-38,*

Scherer, K. R., & Wallbott, H.G. (1994). *Evidence for universality and cultural variation of differential emotion response patterning. Journal of Personality and Social Psychology, 66, 310-328.*

Scherer, K. R. (1997). *Profiles of emotion-antecedent appraisal: testing theoretical predictions across cultures. Cognition and Emotion, 11, 113-150.*

Stefano Baccianella, Andrea Esuli, and Fabrizio Sebastiani.2008. *SENTIWORDNET 3.0: An Enhanced Lexical Resource for Sentiment Analysis and Opinion Mining*

Strapparava, C. and Valitutti, A. 2004. *Wordnet-affect: an affective extension of wordnet. In 4th LREC, pp. 1083-1086*

Takamura Hiroya, Takashi Inui, and Manabu Okumura. 2005. Extracting semantic orientations of words using spin model. In *Proceedings of the 43rd Annual Meeting of the Association for Computational Linguistics(ACL'05)*, pages 133–140.

Wiebe, J., Wilson, T. and Cardie, C. 2005. *Annotating expressions of opinions and emotions in language. LRE, vol. 39(2-3), pp. 165-210.*

http://wordnet.princeton.edu

http://www.cs.waikato.ac.nz/ml/weka/

http://emotion-research.net/toolbox/toolboxdatabase.2006-10-13.2581092615

http://www.affective-sciences.org/researchmaterial

Author Index

Association for Computational Linguistics
209 N. Eighth Street
Stroudsburg, Pennsylvania 18360

CURRAN ASSOCIATES INC.
proceedings.com

ISBN 978-1-5108-0954-3
9 781510 809543